UNDERWATER
ARCHAEOLOGY

UNDERWATER ARCHAEOLOGY

P. E. CLEATOR

Illustrated
Diagrams and Maps by the Author

ST. MARTIN'S PRESS
NEW YORK

AFFILIATED PUBLISHERS Macmillan & Company, Limited, London —
also at Bombay, Calcutta, Madras and Melbourne — The Macmillan
Company of Canada, Limited, Toronto

Contents

To
a certain barber

Illustrations

CHAPTER HEADINGS

1   The Assyrian army crossing a river (as recorded on a bas-relief, now in the British Museum, recovered from the ruins of the Palace of Ashur-nasir-pal at Nineveh).

2   Three pioneers: Paul Bert, Henry Fleuss, John Scott Haldane.

3   The drowned planet (the world ocean as it appears on Goode's homolosine equal-area projection).

4   The walls of Tyre (as depicted on a nineteenth-century engraving).

5   Search patterns.

6   Down among the amphorae (from a photograph).

7   Underwater excavations at Spargi (a sketch based on an original drawing by Laurence Sandy).

8   Plato's Atlantis—plan of the central plain (as depicted in *Critias*).

NUMBERED FIGURES IN TEXT

Author's Note

The study of human antiquities is itself a venerable occupation
—it dates back to the days of Nabonidus and Belshazzar no
less, those last kings of the last dynasty of Babylon. Nabonidus,
however, was essentially a collector of relics, and archaeology,
as opposed to mere antiquarianism, did not emerge as a fully
fledged scientific discipline until as recently as the turn of the
present century, by which time there was a general acceptance
of the painstaking methods of enquiry introduced and developed by Flinders Petrie and A. H. Pitt-Rivers from 1880
onwards. It was they who first laid stress on the potential value
of seeming trivialities, who demonstrated the importance of
stratification, who emphasized the significance of associated
finds, and who insisted upon the need for detailed and accurate
recording—a meticulous approach which remains the basis of
sound excavatory work to this day.

Until the 1940s, such field activities were almost exclusively
confined to the land surface of the globe, though the existence
of a number of underwater sites of historic interest was known,
several of which had been subjected to preliminary surveying
operations, accompanied on occasion by some retrieving of
artifacts. These recoveries, however, represented little more
than a haphazard salvaging of objects, and the problem of how
to conduct a thorough *in situ* examination of a submerged
location remain unanswered, thanks to the hostile nature of the
surrounding medium.

It was this juncture that the advent of the Cousteau–Gagnan
aqualung provided would-be investigators with a portable
breathing device which permitted complete freedom of
movement under water, an indispensable prerequisite not
enjoyed by users of the conventional inflated suit with its
copper helmet, its weighted boots, and its air-line attachment.
A vast new domain, hitherto the preserve of the professional

diver, was thus made readily available to students of man's past, a domain replete with a picturesque vocabulary peculiarly its own—no-stop curve, scuba, nitrogen narcosis, squeezes and nips, not to mention the bends, the chokes, the niggles, the staggers, *et al.*

While an understanding of this terminology need not here concern the uninitiated, it may be noted in passing that among the experts there has been much discussion, revealing a wide divergence of opinion, about the question of what distinguishing name—if any—should be given to this extension of archaeological research. George F. Bass, of the University of Pennsylvania Museum, who has himself actively engaged in submarine excavation, has sought to end the debate by insisting that archaeology is simply archaeology, no matter in what circumstances it happens to be conducted. And while he concedes that in the past its practitioners have frequently been identified in terms of particular cultural, chronological, and geographic areas of interest (hence Egyptologists, Assyriologists, and the like), he goes on to insist that no archaeologist specializes in the environment in which he works. There is, that is to say, no such thing as a mountain archaeologist or a jungle archaeologist.

Two points would seem to be of some relevance here. One is that the sacrosanctity of established custom is always open to challenge, the other that so long as archaeology remained more or less exclusively a land-based activity, the question of environmental specialization did not seriously arise. Today, however, this is no longer the case, and thanks to the radical change in surroundings which investigation of an underwater site involves, not to mention the novel techniques which the work entails, it would appear that the bestowal of some distinguishing label is not merely desirable, but that it has become a practical necessity. Evidence in support of this, at all events, is provided by a recent work on the subject by Dr. Bass himself. For although he has been careful to employ the title *Archaeology Under Water,* he nevertheless finds it convenient to make constant reference to underwater archaeology in the text!

The use of such a description, needless to say, in no way invalidates the dictum that, under water or on land, archaeology is archaeology—it has but to be asked where, if separate and distinct activities are involved, the one begins and the other ends. For although some land sites are to be found on the tops of mountains, and many underwater sites in the depths of the sea, there are borderline examples which belong to neither category. Are the peat bogs of Scandinavia, for instance, renowned as the source of well preserved human remains (such as those of the Tollund Man), to be looked upon as a land or an underwater site? And what of the operations conducted in Denmark's Roskilde Fjord, where five Viking block ships, found lying in shallow water, were enclosed by a coffer-dam and the sea pumped out, leaving the vessels high and dry?

Because underwater archaeology differs from its land-based counterpart only in some of its methods, the compilers of the British Sub Aqua Club's official *Diving Manual* express a preference for the description 'Nautical Archaeology' or 'Archaeology of the Sea and Inland Waters'. But if, in search of an acceptable title, we dismiss this last (as we surely must) on the grounds that it lacks conciseness, and just as firmly reject all adjectival expressions (nautical, marine, submarine) which, because they appertain to the sea alone, exclude fresh water sites; and if we also dispense with barbarisms such as 'Aque-ology' and 'Hydroarchaeology', we are left with a choice between 'Subaqueous' and 'Underwater'. In the absence of what the author regards as a suitable alternative, 'Underwater Archaeology' has accordingly been selected for use throughout the pages which follow.

Acknowledgements

Literature consulted during the writing of this book includes such standard works of reference as Americana, Britannica, Caxton's, Chambers's, Collier's, Columbia, Compton's, Everyman's, Funk and Wagnall's, Grolier's, Richard's, Universal, the *Diving Manual* of the British Sub-Aqua Club, S.N.A.P.'s *Guide to Practical Marine Archaeology*, and sundry issues of the American Journal of Archaeology, the *National Geographic Magazine*, and *Forma Maris Antiqui*, in addition to the items listed in the Bibliography, which last have been numbered so as to facilitate identification where a particular author is mentioned in the text. As for the task of tracing and providing copies of many of these volumes, it finds me heavily indebted to an anonymous army of librarians, resident both at home and abroad.

Much valuable information, based on their personal experience of archaeological activities under water, has come from my meetings and discussions with Miss Joan du Plat Taylor, of the Committee for Nautical Archaeology at the University of London's Institute of Archaeology, and with Dr. George F. Bass, of the University of Pennsylvania Museum, and also from correspondence I have had with other leading exponents— Professor Nino Lamboglia, Director of the *Centro Sperimentale di Archeologia Sottomarina*, Albenga; Frédéric Dumas and Commander Philippe Tailliez, of the *Groupe d'Étude et de Recherches Sous-Marines*, Toulon; Lieutenant-Commander Alan Bax, of the School for Nautical Archaeology, Plymouth (S.N.A.P.); Henri Broussard, of the *Club Alpin Sous-Marin*, Cannes; Dr. Michael L. Katzef, Assistant Professor of the Department of Art, Oberlin College, Ohio; W. E. Berg, of the National Aeronautics and Space Council, Washington; and Sidney Wignall, leader of the 'Spanish Armada Salvage Expedition', Old Colwyn. I am also obliged for the ready response to requests for assistance given by Henri Broussard's associate Y. de Rolland-Dalon, by Charles A. Furth and R. Eames, of George Allen & Unwin, by J. D. 'Ors, of the American Museum of Natural History, by Michael Dolley, of the Department of Modern History at the Queen's University of Belfast, by Mrs. E. Tucker, of the National Maritime Museum, Greenwich, by members of the North American Rockwell Corporation, Long Beach, California, by the editors of the magazines *Profile*, *L'Europeo*, and *Mondo Sommerso*, and by Rolf Blomberg, now once again resident in Quito, and so within reach of his beloved Amazonia.

The provision of photographic material once again finds me beholden to Dr. Bass, as well as to Mendel L. Peterson, Director of the Underwater Exploration Project of the Smithsonian Institution, Washington, to the Statens Sjöhistoriska Museum, Stockholm, to the National Museum, Le Bardo, Tunis, to the National Archaeological Museum, Athens, to the British Museum, to Scott Aviation, Lancaster, New York, and to Siebe Gorman and Company, Chessington. The last-named also kindly assented to my making free use of sketches relating to the early history of diving which appear in Sir Robert H. Davis' monumental *Deep Diving and Submarine Operations*. As to this, in the interest of accuracy, these and other line illustrations have been re-drawn from reproductions of original engravings, or from photographic prints, as elsewhere acknowledged.

Production, to the accompaniment of sage suggestions and useful advice, has once again been the concern of Gordon Chesterfield and his colleagues, though not, alas, of my old friend W. H. Browning, M.A., recently deceased. Since his Oxford days the possessor of an unrivalled knowledge of the intricacies of the English language, and after serving for the past forty years as a sort of personal H. W. Fowler, he will proof-read for me no more. Before these words could make their way into print, he collapsed and died while dining with convivial companions. So while I mourn his passing, there is at any rate no need to lament the manner of his end.

P. E. CLEATOR

Introduction

Man inhabits a potentially drowned planet, three-quarters covered by water in such quantity that were it not for the presence of crustal irregularities, its entire surface area would be submerged to a depth of $1\frac{1}{2}$ miles—a circumstance which raises important issues for the underwater archaeologist. Is this a state of affairs which has existed at any time in the past? What is the source of so vast an accumulation of enveloping liquid? Is it still being produced in significant amounts?

The answer to the question of source, at all events in the ultimate analysis, is not far to seek. Water consists of 2 atoms of hydrogen in association with 1 atom of oxygen; the atomic (relative) weights of the two gases are respectively 1 and 16; hence some 150,000,000,000,000,000 tons of the one must have entered into chemical combination with 1,200,000,000,000,000,000 tons of the other to produce the fluid content of the world's seas, conservatively estimated to weigh a total of no less than $1,350 \times 10^{15}$ tons. Doubtless the process was a gradual one, and while it is true that, on ignition, a hydrogen–oxygen mixture detonates violently, it is also the case that a jet of hydrogen will burn quietly and uneventfully in an atmosphere of oxygen (and *vice versa*) to furnish water. Moreover, such direct synthesis, explosively or otherwise, need not necessarily have been involved, as water is also one of the products of innumerable other chemical processes, as when aluminium oxide combines with hydrochloric acid, or chlorate compounds are reduced to chlorides.

Within the molten mass of a newly formed earth, many such reactions must have taken place, to the accompaniment of much internal agitation, by no means yet abated. Thus the motive force of vulcanism is essentially water in gaseous form, and during an eruption steam is emitted in amounts which cannot be regarded as other than impressive. If the whole of this aqueous product were juvenile, i.e., if it had not previously formed part of the hydrosphere, measurements and calculations have shown the scale of emission to be sufficient to double the contents of the ocean within a relatively short period. Such an increase has clearly not taken place within the time limit imposed by the estimated annual output, and all the indications are that the total quantity of terrestrial surface water (in solid, liquid, or gaseous form) has changed but little during the past thousand or so million years. Seemingly, then, what promotes much of today's vulcanism is the seepage underground of surface water from supplies which are already existing—heavy rainfall, to some extent, but mainly from an oceanic source, a supposition which finds support in the circumstance that most of the world's still active volcanoes are situated near the sea, if they are not actually located beneath it.

As for the question of whether or not the earth has at any time been a completely drowned planet, there is no evidence of this, one way or the other. It may be supposed, however, that in the years following its birth, the eventual appearance of an igneous crust was accompanied by the release of clouds of steam, and that as the temperature continued to moderate, these clouds condensed and produced showers, thus still further assisting the cooling process and making possible the formation of lakes and seas. What followed, according to the classical conception of the earth as a once molten and continuously cooling globe subject to internal shrinkage, was that this contraction ultimately left the solidified outer shell insufficiently supported. For its part, the newly formed crust retained its rigidity until the stress became too great, whereupon it began to crack and break-up, raising vast mountains of contorted rock as it adjusted itself to the contours of the diminishing interior. The situation then remained comparatively stable until collapse was once again threatened, so that progress has been marked by alternate periods of catastrophic activity and of relative calm, which last state the earth appears to be experiencing at the moment. Thus at the present time, indications of crustal instability, as exemplified by volcanic activity and earthquakes, are more or less restricted to certain well defined regions, notably to the length of the western coastal fringe of the two Americas, and thence by way of Alaska to Japan, the Philippines, and Indonesia (the circum-Pacific belt, by far the worst affected area), and to a Mediterranean-trans-Asiatic belt, extending from North Africa through Spain and Italy to India and Burma, by way of Greece, Turkey, and Iran. But although the presence of volcanoes denotes a locality where earthquakes are also liable to occur, neither phenomenon is regarded as being the cause (or the effect) of the other. Each, however, is believed to be intimately associated with the existence of fracture zones in the vicinity of geologically recent mountain chains.

But the orthodox view, based on the Kelvin dictum that since its formation, the earth has been living on an ever dwindling amount of internal heat bequeathed to it by the sun, has since been upset by the discovery of radio-activity among rocks, and by the realization that such a process of spontaneous decay provides the earth with a built-in heat source of its own. This situation, it has been held, not only accounts for the fact that surface conditions on earth belie any suggestion that, since the formation of the seas, there has been any appreciable cooling down, but it also calls into question the worth of the theory of crustal collapse as the prime cause of mountain-building, the more so as this fails satisfactorily to account for the present disposition of the continents. It has even been conjectured that the earth, thanks to internal thermonuclear activity, has for long been generating heat at a faster pace than it was losing it. Thus, in 1933, O. C. Hilgenberg pictured a globe which, far from shrinking, was in fact expanding! In its original form, this startling proposal involved the highly suspect notion of a gain in terrestrial mass, but soon afterwards the idea was placed on a more scientifically acceptable basis by the astronomer J. K. E. Halm, who sought to account for any increase in the earth's volume by postulating a much higher initial density (9·13, on average) than that which now obtains (5·5). His calculations favoured an original mean radius of 3,372 miles, as compared with the present figure of 3,956 miles.

Highly improbable though the idea of an expanding earth may at first appear, it has been urged on its behalf that it at least provides possible answers to more problems than it raises, and it now claims a number of reputable geologists among its advocates. It throws some light, for example, upon the otherwise puzzling circumstance that instead of the relatively light sialic material of the crustal region being spread uniformly over the earth's surface, as might have been expected, it is found to be concentrated in the up-lifted land masses (a fact which, of course, helps to explain their elevated state). Might not this highly selective distribution be accounted for by supposing that a slow but continuous process of expansion first cracked the earth's crust, and then caused an ever-increasing separation of rudimentary continents, a dispersal influenced by the sluggish movement of convection currents in the under-lying mantle?

It will be manifest that geologic concepts such as those which relate to earth movements and changes in sea level are of particular concern to the underwater archaeologist, as these occurrences, if of sufficiently recent date, may well have resulted in the submergence of human handiwork. And while there has been much criticism, not infrequently accompanied by outright rejection, of such revolutionary theories as those of an expanding earth, internal convection currents, and continental drift (this last a notion advanced by A. Snider as long ago as 1858), a final verdict on the worth and interdependence of these far-reaching ideas is still awaited. In the meantime, and however fixed and immoveable the continental land masses may appear to be, there can be no disputing that they are continuously subject to compensatory movements in which subsidence alternates with up-lift, in an effort to achieve that condition of equilibrium to which the American geologist C. E. Dutton gave the name isostasy. The phenomenon thus named is based on the principle that equal masses of terrestrial matter underlie equal areas, and it has in fact been demonstrated (by gravimetric means) that the thickness of the earth's crust is much greater under elevated peaks than it is under the sea. The height of a mountain, that is to say, is offset by the depth of its root, so that, as its topmost substance is gradually eroded by weathering and the load on its foundations steadily decreases, the edifice slowly rises. Conversely, adjacent regions upon which debris from the denuded highlands is deposited begin to sink under the constantly added weight, thereby assisting in the restoration of isostatic balance.

Convincing proof of the uplifting of land is afforded by the presence of sedimentary (i.e., water-laid) rocks at the summit of some of the world's highest mountains, including Mount

Everest, where terrain that once formed the bottom of the ocean has been raised to a height of more than five miles. Similar movements, though on a less spectacular scale, are indicated by the sight of old strand lines, running at an acute angle. But the relationship between land and sea is by no means a one-sided affair, for it is also affected by alterations in water level. In effect, the situation which exists at any given time and place is governed by the fact that not only the land, but also the level of the sea, may be rising, static, or subsiding. Nor is this all, for if both land and sea happen to be rising (or falling) simultaneously, the question of rate is clearly of importance, as in such circumstances, one of these activities will almost certainly be gaining on the other. As a general rule, vertical land movements are slow and regional, whereas changes in sea level tend to be comparatively rapid and are uniform the world over, i.e., they are absolute or eustatic. Even so, when an ancient marine terrace is found high above the reach of any waves, it is not always easy to determine whether it owes its present location to the fact that the land has been raised, or that the ocean has receded, or to a combination of the two.

Insofar as the underwater archaeologist is concerned, and apart from the fact that contraction of the earth's surface would cause sea levels to rise, while expansion would have the opposite effect, there are a number of other ways in which such a rise or fall might be brought about without any substantial increase or decrease in the total amount of the water content of the ocean. Thus displacement by sedimentation would cause the sea to rise, as would its expansion occasioned by an increase in temperature. The converse is also the case, and what has undoubtedly brought about the greatest changes in sea level in geologically recent times has been the periodic advance and retreat of the Polar ice caps. In the course of the past million years, enormous quantities of water have been extracted from, and subsequently returned to, the oceans and seas in a series of refrigerative movements which have been identified in Alpine Europe (and whose North American equivalents are shown in parenthesis) as the Gunz (Nebraskan), Mindel (Kansan), Riss (Illinoian), and Würm (Wisconsin) glaciations.

Investigations have been made into the effect of these

successive Ice Ages on ocean levels, and falls of up to 400 feet postulated. Unexpectedly, clear indications have also been found that after each melting of the ice sheets, the sea has consistently failed to return to its previous level, a puzzling circumstance which, failing an ever-growing retention of water in frozen form (which does not appear to be the answer) can only be explained on the assumption that the volume of the ocean basins has increased, with particular reference to the Pacific, much of the floor of which appears to be sinking.

The last (and less severe) Würm-Wisconsin glaciation would seem to have brought about a fall in the sea of some 200 feet, whereafter a steady rise in water levels continued to take place until some 6,000 years ago, since when there has been a marked slowing down. As for the future, the trend of events remains uncertain, and the question of whether we are still in the process of leaving the last Ice Age behind, or are already heading for the next, cannot yet be answered. The fact is that the causes of glaciation are still far from being understood, though they have long been assumed to be climatic. Variations in the amount of solar heat received by the earth (perhaps attributable to sunspot activity, or to the amount of carbon dioxide in the atmosphere) have been suggested as exercising a decisive influence, in support of which it has been pointed out that whereas at the present time a mean temperature of 9·4 degrees C. which prevails in the Swiss Alps suffices to halt glaciers at an altitude of 3,400 feet, an average temperature fall of only 5 degrees would bring the ice down to the banks of Lake Geneva, a descent of 1,500 feet.

Meanwhile, as water levels continue their slow rise, enormous quantities of ice still remain in cold storage in the polar regions —an estimated 4,500,000 cubic miles of it, nine-tenths of which is to be found in the Antarctic. It has also been calculated that if all the water thus locked up were to be restored to the sea, its level could rise by as much as 250 feet, though because of compensatory isostatic effects, the actual figure would be about half this. For one thing, not only would the weight of added water depress the ocean floor, but the crustal material so displaced would be forced under the continents, causing them to rise. And for another, the removal of the immense ice burden from Antarctica and other regions (amounting, in all, to more than a tenth of the earth's land surface) would also result in their being uplifted. Such a process of isostatic re-elevation is, in fact, still taking place at the present time, an aftermath of the retreat of the last European and North American ice sheets. Observations have shown that with the passing of each century, land at the northern end of the Gulf of Bosnia is raised by another yard out of the height of 700 feet it has yet to attain before equilibrium is established. Similarly, thanks to the disappearance of their northern ice covering, the British Isles now display a pronounced tilt, with parts of Scotland rising at a rate of four inches each century, and the coasts of southern England sinking by a similar amount. The implication is that, failing the taking of effective preventative measures, in the not too remote future London is likely to find itself awash.

Ultimately, of course, in the event of a contemplated rise in sea level exceeding 100 feet, other great cities of the world would vanish beneath the waves, and so become of concern to underwater archaeologists of the future. In the meantime, it was during what the geologists have distinguished as the Quaternary or fourth great period of the earth's history that the aforementioned series of glaciations chanced to coincide with the emergence of mankind, so that the periodic advance and retreat of the ice sheets must have had a profound effect upon the way of life of our primitive ancestors. At all events, within the past 25,000 years, a fall in sea level in the vicinity of the Bering Strait provided a land bridge between what is now Siberia and Alaska, permitting a migration of Asiatic peoples from the Old World to the New, until melting ice and rising waters brought the traffic to a halt, or at any rate greatly slowed it down. Other lands separated by straits where the water is relatively shallow, and which at various times in the recent past must also have been connected, include India-Ceylon, Siberia–Japan, Australia–New Guinea, and France–England. Doubtless men once inhabited and roamed the areas now under water, and so witnessed their gradual flooding. And somewhere, perhaps, awaiting discovery, there yet exists a set of inundated cave drawings, depicting the scene. . . .

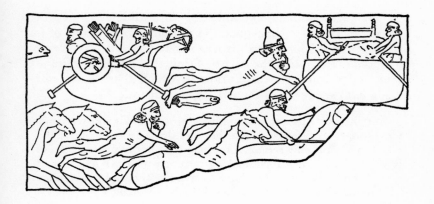

Chapter One

Advent of the Aqualung

I

A prerequisite of an archaeological investigation conducted under water is an ability to make an extended stay in the vicinity of the site, and this, in turn, calls for the use of some form of breathing apparatus. Without resort to artificial aids, even if no great depth is attained and no undue exertion is made (both of which entail an increase in the rate of consumption of the limited supply of oxygen contained in the lungs), somewhat less than five minutes is normally to be regarded as the maximum of human endurance. Moreover, while sponge and pearl divers, naked and unequipped, have engaged in their hazardous pursuit since time immemorial, more often than not it has been to the great and lasting detriment of their health. For if certain necessary precautions are not strictly observed, the effects of water pressure can be highly deleterious, and down through the centuries, uncomprehending harvesters of the sea-bed have acquired an unenviable reputation for avoiding a palsied middle or old age, only by the remedial expedient of dying young.

As was to be expected, meanwhile, other uses for the skills of the diver soon came to be found, notably in times of war (as

Homer,[75] Herodotus,[71] Pausanias,[104] Thucydides,[137] and other authorities recount), and once the military applications of his art had been demonstrated, it was inevitable that ways should be sought of extending the length of time that could be gainfully spent under water, an aspiration to which there is an early (*c.* 360 B.C.) reference in the writings of Aristotle:[2]

> Just then as divers are sometimes provided with instruments for respiration, through which they can draw air from above the water, and thus may remain for a long time under the sea, so also have elephants been furnished by nature with their lengthened nostril; and whenever they have to traverse through water, they lift this up above the surface and breathe through it.

This mention of elephants and of the usefulness of a breathing tube finds an echo in Pliny,[108] some four and a half centuries later, whereafter the idea of underwater swimmers providing themselves with a supply of air by way of a pipe line, one end of which was held in the mouth, while the other terminated in a float at the surface, was hopefully advocated by a long succession

1. Proposed breathing tube and surface float, from the Codex Atlanticus *of Leonardo da Vinci (1452–1519)*

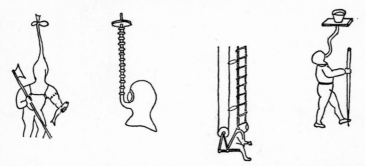

2. *Underwater breathing equipment as envisaged (left to right) by Vegetius (1511), Vallo (1524), Lorini (1597), and Robert Fludd (1617).*

of armchair divers in the years which followed, the usually more discerning Leonardo da Vinci among them.

It was not until the start of the seventeenth century that serious doubts about the feasibility of the proposal began to arise, thanks to a belated appreciation of the fact that the earth's atmosphere was possessed of weight (which diminished with altitude), and to the realization that water, with a density about 900 times that of air, must exert a much greater pressure on objects immersed in it—a pressure, moreover, which steadily increased with depth. So it came about that in 1681, in a treatise entitled 'The Art of Breathing Under Water', Jean de Hautefeuille was able effectively to dispose of the time-honoured notion that an open ended breathing tube could be employed to sustain a deep-sea-diver:

> A man's lungs are a sort of bellows and in order to inflate them the man must raise the column of water which is pressing down on him from above. However, this column being very heavy and the strength of his muscles being very inadequate he finds he cannot raise the column of water and therefore he cannot breathe.

In practice, it has since been shown that the usefulness of a mouth-to-air breathing device is strictly limited—it cannot be made to operate below depths which are to be measured in inches rather than in feet. Beyond this, the constrictive effect of the weight of air-plus-water on the submerged body of a swimmer whose lungs are in direct communication with the

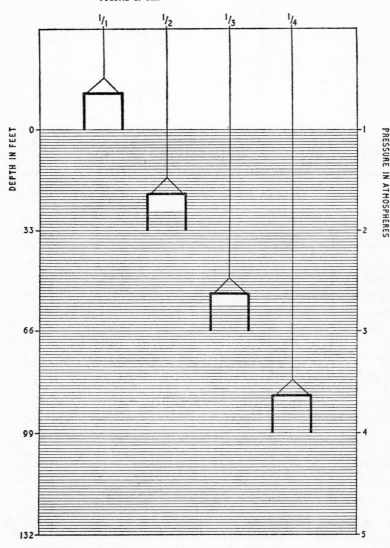

VOLUME OF AIR

$1/_1$ $1/_2$ $1/_3$ $1/_4$

DEPTH IN FEET

PRESSURE IN ATMOSPHERES

0 — 1

33 — 2

66 — 3

99 — 4

132 — 5

3. In accordance with Boyle's Law, the volume of air contained in a diving bell varies inversely with the pressure to which it is subjected.

atmosphere makes respiration impossible. But this is not to say, of course, that the problem of sustained breathing under water is insoluble. The answer is to eliminate any difference in air pressure between the user and his source of supply, and a means of accomplishing this has long been available in the guise of the diving bell. When such a contrivance is lowered into water, care being taken to maintain it in an upright position, the pressure of the air trapped inside it automatically adjusts itself to that of its fluid surroundings.

As it happened, in de Hautefeuille's day the subject of air pressure and its equalization had recently been investigated by Robert Boyle, who in the course of his experiments contrived to balance the weight exerted by the atmosphere against a quantity of mercury contained in a glass tube. In so doing, he found that the weight of the one was matched by a column of the other which measured 29·9 inches (760 mm) in length. This figure, which may also be expressed as 14·7 pounds per square inch, has since been adopted as the unit of pressure in underwater practice, and is referred to as 1 atmosphere—the equivalent of 33 feet of salt (34 feet of fresh) water.*

As a result of his investigations, Boyle was able to enunciate a general principle (the Law which now bears his name) relating to the behaviour of gases. This asserts that, subject to the maintenance of a uniform temperature, the volume of a given quantity of a gas varies inversely as the pressure, a statement which may be expressed algebraically as

$$pv = K,$$

where p = pressure, v = volume, and K = a constant.

This is merely a concise way of saying that when the pressure is doubled, the volume is halved. Or, translated into terms applicable to the diving bell, it indicates that when such a vessel is lowered into the sea to a depth of 33 feet, the pressure of the air inside it (which stood, initially, at 1 atmosphere) will be increased to 2 atmospheres, while its volume will be reduced by half, an ingress of water occupying the vacated space. Assuming the descent to continue, at a depth of $2 \times 33 = 66$

*Depth gauges used by divers usually indicate water pressure only, giving a reading which is referred to as gauge pressure, in order to distinguish it from total or absolute pressure which also takes into account the added weight of the earth's blanket of air. Thus, in terms of atmospheres, absolute pressure is equal to gauge pressure plus 1.

feet the air, now under a pressure of 3 atmospheres, will be compressed to a third of its original volume, and so on, as the following tabulation shows:

Depth in feet	0	33	66	99	132	$n-1 \times 33$
Absolute pressure in atmospheres	1	2	3	4	5	n
Volume of air	1/1	1/2	1/3	1/4	1/5	$1/n$

It may be safely assumed that these and other technical aspects of the diving bell were of small concern to its early users, and significant improvements in design (associated with the names of Franz Kessler, Denis Papin, Edmund Halley, and Charles Spalding, among others) had to await the start of the seventeenth century. At the same time, the evident limitations of the device inspired attempts to produce a form of protective

4. Development of the diving bell. In 1616, Franz Kessler (left) devised a man-sized bell complete with viewing windows and a buoyancy regulator (in the form of ballast) which enabled the occupant to walk about the sea-bed. By the end of the century, Edmund Halley, of comet fame, had produced the more sophisticated apparatus shown on the right, from which the user could emerge and make an underwater excursion.

apparel which, while it enabled the wearer to breathe under water, would also allow him greater freedom of movement. Two methods of achieving this suggested themselves, given the need to avoid any difference in pressure between the wearer's immediate surroundings and his air supply. One was constantly to maintain the air within the suit at a pressure equal to that exerted by the water (which steadily increased with depth), the other to resort to a sealed and rigid container, thereby ensuring that, irrespective of external influences, the air within the dress remained at (or near) atmospheric pressure at all times (as in the case of underwater craft such as the submarine).

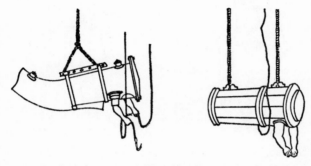

5. *Early eighteenth century rigid type of diving outfit, as devised by John Lethbridge (left) and Captain Rowe (right).*

At any rate in theory, the rigid type of covering offered the very considerable advantage that the production of excessive air pressures (with its attendant problems and hazards) was unnecessary. But in practice, as a certain John Lethbridge and other would-be exponents soon discovered, their leather and timber outfits were neither designed nor built to withstand the water pressures which were to be encountered beyond all but the most modest of depths, and this problem was not overcome until there was resort to metal construction, incorporating the use of articulated joints. But although such armoured suits made possible descents of 400 feet and more, it was found that at these depths the moveable joints of the outfit tended to become so constricted as to render them unworkable, with the result that the wearer was denied effective use of his limbs.

In effect, while such suits could be relied upon to offer immunity from extremes of pressure, they did so at the cost of
mobility. The price of success, that is to say, was failure. . . .

Attention, meanwhile, was also being given to the problems
associated with the development of a pressurized suit, in the
shape of a flexible dress which could be inflated with air
delivered to it from the surface, a desideratum which was
finally achieved by a naturalized British citizen named
Augustus Siebe. On his arrival in London in 1816, and after a

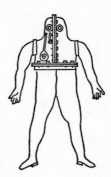

*6. Leather diving dress, complete with helmet, produced in 1797 by
K. H. Klingert (left). Twin breathing tubes led to a surface float, an
arrangement which precluded all but the most shallow of dives, as a trial
immersion in the waters of the Oder River promptly demonstrated. Then
in 1802, William Forder (right) sought to make good this deficiency by
designing a suit which was to be inflated by operating a pair of bellows.
But although in theory this pressurising procedure was sound, the proposed method of implementing it proved inadequate.*

period of employment as an instrument maker, the newcomer
set up in business on his own account (in which enterprise he
was joined by his son-in-law, W. A. Gorman), and turned his
inventive genius to the devising of such varied items as a breech-
loading rifle, a paper-making machine, a hydraulic pump—
and a diving suit. At the time, there was in use a simple metal
helmet, fitted with a glass face plate and a couple of pipes, one
(by means of which air was pumped in) extending to the surface,
the other a much shorter version (through which used air
made its escape). Siebe's first move was to attach to the helmet

a waterproof jacket which reached down to the diver's waist. The covering remained open at the bottom (cf. the diving bell) so that air pumped into the helmet under pressure could escape freely at the lower level.

This so-called 'open' dress was introduced in 1819, and later demonstrated its usefulness when it was successfully used in the salvaging of cannon and other equipment from the wreck of H.M.S. *Royal George*, which had capsized and sunk at Spithead half a century earlier. It was at this juncture (1837), in the light of considerable operational experience, that the 'open' dress was modified and transformed into the now familiar 'closed' type of outfit, as worn by professional divers at the present time. In its original form, users of Siebe's 'open' outfit needed to maintain an upright position, lest water should flood in, and it was in an effort to overcome this serious restriction on a diver's movements that the inventor introduced what, to those granted wisdom after the event, appears to be the obvious remedy of providing a sealed suit, in the form of an airtight garment which (with the exception of the hands) enclosed the wearer completely. As a safety measure, the dress was fitted with non-return inlet and outlet valves, the one ensuring that in the event of damage to the air supply line (or to the pump feeding it), the highly pressurized air in the suit was prevented from escaping whence it came, the other freely permitting the departure of exhaled air without allowing a back-flow of water.

In 1840, divers who in the previous year had begun the task of placing explosive charges in the hull of the *Royal George*, that the wreck of the vessel might be disposed of by blowing it up, made use of the new dress for the first time. They at once acclaimed it an outstanding success, an opinion evidently shared by the Lord Commissioners of the Admiralty who, after paying an official visit to the scene of operations in August of that year, subsequently expressed

their decided approbation of Mr. Siebe's diving helmet and dress which combine so many improvements; a principal feature of which is, the diver can descend head foremost with safety . . .

II

The introduction of Augustus Siebe's 'closed' dress constituted a decisive turning point in the history of man's underwater aspirations. From 1837 onwards, as well as making good his escape from the confines of the diving bell, he also found himself free to move about the sea-bed without being in imminent danger of drowning. And the reliability and intrinsic worth of the new costume have since been shown by the fact that, a century and a half later, it remains basically unaltered and has become firmly established as the standard equipment of the professional salvor.

Even so, it has long been recognized that the conventional diving dress imposes irksome limitations upon the activities of the wearer, for the outfit is bulky and hence cumbersome, and this necessarily restricts lateral movement. So does the fact that the user is at all times tethered to a source of air at the surface, and that he must venture warily into enclosed spaces, lest his air-pipe or his life-line suffers entanglement. Again, ownership of the outfit is usually the prerogative of commercial undertakings, as it is expensive to purchase and even more costly to employ and maintain, requiring as it does much ancillary equipment, including major items such as a supply boat fitted with pumps or a compressor, not to mention a trained staff in constant attendance. And yet, at any rate in theory, there is a simple way out of this situation—all that is necessary is to furnish the diver with a self-contained underwater breathing apparatus,* so ending his dependence on atmospheric air, and leaving him free to move about as he pleases.

Such a prospect is undoubtedly an inviting one, and down through the centuries the idea has received its due share of attention from would-be exponents. In terms of years, its beginnings have ostensibly been traced as far back as the Assyrians (*c.* 900 B.C.) on evidence extracted from bas-reliefs which Henry Layard recovered from the ruins of the palace of Ashur-nasir-pal at Nineveh. A drawing based on one of

---

*Hence SCUBA, an imprecise acronym variously attributed to J. Y. Cousteau by A. P. Balder[6] and to members of a Washington diving group by James Dugan,[48] who makes the point that the more definitive term 'air lung' (as opposed to 'oxygen lung') is greatly to be preferred. He also vouchsafes the information that the trade name 'Aqualung' was coined by one Henri Dolisie, of Montreal.

7. Part of an Assyrian bas-relief recovered from the ruins of the Palace of Ashur-nasir-pal at Nineveh (c. 900 B.C.). One of the swimmers would appear to be making use of what has been held to be an underwater breathing device. But see Chapter Heading and text reference.

these carvings (here reproduced) depicts what appears to be a man swimming under water, with his air supply contained in an inflated goatskin strapped to his chest, from which container a tube extends to his mouth. But what at first sight seems to be the obvious interpretation is not to be so regarded, as R. H. Davis[41] has convincingly argued. Thus it may be accepted that what the illustration shows is one of a group of surface swimmers in the act of crossing a river with the assistance of the Assyrian equivalent of a life-jacket—if only because a bag of air would render the user unsinkable as, indeed, was its intended purpose. Again, the fact that one of the legs of the animal skin appears to be held in the mouth of the voyager suggest that, far from receiving a stream of air from it, from time to time he may have found it necessary to make good a loss of buoyancy by blowing into it! Nor, it would seem, is the fact that the alleged diver is shown in the company of fish to be regarded as anything more significant than an example of artistic licence, especially when it is realized that the scene has been taken out of a context which depicts companions of the swimmer making the crossing in boats (*vide* Chapter Heading).

In the event, it was not until the start of the fifteenth century A.D. that a German engineer, Konrad Kyeser von Eichstädt, proposed the use of diving equipment consisting of a leather jacket surmounted by a metal globe, both of which components were lined with sponge 'to retain the air', while from the top of the helmet there sprouted a length of tube which terminated in an air-bag. About 1450, the essentials of this somewhat dubious arrangement were advocated by the Italian Giacomo Mariano (*alias* Taccola), who, by way of simplification, reduced the outfit to a form of nosebag, in which air was to be stored. And after another interval of half a century, Leonardo da Vinci also gave his attention to the requirements of a self-contained underwater appliance, of which he sketched several versions. One of these was in the guise of a combined face mask and air reservoir, the lower part of which found support on the

8. *Diving costumes as conceived by Giacomo Mariano (top), Leonardo da Vinci (centre), and Giovanni Borelli (bottom). Note the foot-fins advocated (in 1680) by the last-named.*

chest of the wearer, while another design featured this item as part of a complete diving dress. These and similar proposals may be regarded as culminating in the idea of Giovanni Alfonso Borelli, put forward in a posthumous work published in Rome in 1680. In it the author suggested that the diver be garbed in a leather costume complete with an extra-large metal helmet containing air at atmospheric pressure, the wearer inhaling through the nose and breathing out by way of the mouth. A curved pipe conveyed his exhalations to a leather bag, whence they were returned to the helmet—cooled, purified, and in a state which was hopefully held to be fit for re-breathing!

The weakness of all these proposals is attributable in no small measure to the fact that they were made at a time when little or nothing was known about the character of air, let alone the mechanics of respiration, though John Mayow had recently (1674) demonstrated the composite nature of the atmosphere by confining a mouse in a bell-jar over water. He observed that the imprisoned animal's breathing brought about a diminution in the volume of the air in the jar, and that the gas which remained was no longer capable of supporting life. But it was not until the latter part of the eighteenth century that air was shown to consist of a mixture of two principal gases, together with traces of others. Of these, it was the presence of one of the lesser items—carbon dioxide—which was first established, thanks to the investigations of Joseph Black, a professor of chemistry at Glasgow, who termed his discovery 'fixed air'.

Oxygen, one of the two main constituents, was actually prepared by a number of early experimenters (Eck de Sultzbach, 1489; O. Borch, 1678; S. Hales, 1727; P. Scheele, 1771; P. Payen and J. Priestley, 1774) without their recognizing its atmospheric associations, the credit for which belongs to Antione Laurent Lavoisier. By heating first tin, and then mercury, in air in closed vessels, the French savant, after noting that only some of the air was absorbed by the metals, concluded that it must consist of at least two ingredients. He also observed that the quantity of gas taken up by the mercury amounted to about one sixth (the actual figure is nearer one fifth) of the volume of the air in his apparatus. Moreover, that portion which remained would not support combustion and quickly caused the death of a small rodent placed in it. Lavoisier accordingly termed this residue *azote* (Gk., not, life), by which name it is still known in France. German chemists labelled it *stickstoff* (suffocating stuff), while in Britain it came to be called nitrogen.

At this juncture (the year was 1774), Lavoisier learned of a remarkable gas which Joseph Priestley had obtained by focusing the rays of an outsize burning glass on a quantity of *mercurius calcinatus per se* (red oxide of mercury)—the very substance which had been formed in the course of the Frenchman's own investigations. He accordingly heated some of this material in a retort, and so obtained a supply of the gas which he had earlier induced the metal to absorb. And as Priestley had found, a lighted candle, when immersed in it, burnt with great brilliancy, while a smouldering splinter of wood immediately burst into flame. Lavoisier first referred to this remarkable and unusually active gas as *vital air*, but afterwards re-named it oxygen (Gk., sharp, to generate), in deference to the mistaken belief, then prevalent, that all acids contained it. The designation has nevertheless been retained.

Modern and precise methods of atmospheric analysis, in confirming Lavoisier's findings, have also detected the hitherto unsuspected presence of small quantities of other gases. As a result of thousands of painstaking determinations, made in various parts of the world, the average composition of air has been shown to be:

Per cent of	By weight	By volume
Nitrogen	75·51	78·03
Oxygen	23·15	20·99
Carbon dioxide	0·04	0·03
Other gases	1·30	0·95

Newcomers such as the inert gases (xenon, krypton, neon, helium and argon, of which the last-named largely predominates) were not detected until the 1890s, by which time some understanding had been gained of the respiratory process. This was found to involve what is known as the carbon cycle, in which atmospheric nitrogen, it appeared, acted merely as a diluent to the much more active oxygen. No less vital was the small and seemingly insignificant amount of carbon dioxide, which proved to be the ultimate source of the carbon content of plants and animals, without which terrestrial life as we know it could not exist.

In sunlight (as opposed to shade), plants are able photosynthetically to transform water and the carbon dioxide of the air into free oxygen and complex organic compounds such as starches and sugars. The last-named serve as food for animals, the carbon of whose bodily fats and proteins comes either directly from vegetation which they have eaten, or, in the case of the carnivores, indirectly from the flesh of their herbivorous victims. And animal life, for its part, on breathing the oxygen of the air, converts it into carbon dioxide, and by exhalation returns it to the atmosphere for use by plants, thus completing the round.

Investigation has since revealed that in human respiration, under normal working conditions, the oxygen content of breathed air shows a reduction of 5 per cent., while the amount of carbon dioxide is increased by about 4 per cent. From this, it was evident that in any process of air regeneration suitable for use in a self-contained diving suit, it would be necessary continuously to replace the oxygen at a rate equal to that at which it was being consumed, while at the same time providing some means of absorbing the unwanted carbon dioxide. For this gas, though not inherently poisonous, gives rise to deleterious effects if breathed in amounts of over 5 per cent., while in excess it can cause death by suffocation.

The two essential requirements of an independent diving lung were first successfully applied to a breathing device by the Englishman Henry Fleuss, while serving as an officer in the merchant marine. He began work on his apparatus in 1876, and in due course it emerged as a rubber face mask complete with an inhalation bag, a cylinder of compressed oxygen, and a purification chamber charged with a carbon dioxide absorbent (consisting of tow, impregnated with caustic potash solution). In 1788, this contrivance was offered to, and was taken up by, Siebe Gorman and Company (then) of London, whose R. H. Davis (when he joined the firm four years later), at first in collaboration with the inventor until his retirement, and later on his own initiative, introduced a variety of improved designs for specialized purposes. Several of these subsequently found important wartime applications, from face masks for high altitude flyers to the well known D.S.E.A. (Davis Submerged Escape Apparatus) for use by trapped submarine personnel.

But although the closed-circuit oxygen breathing equipment provides the wearer with a maximum of endurance in return for a minimum of effort, and is particularly valuable militarily for use in underwater activities, since it leaves no tell-tale trail of air bubbles, it was discovered to possess one great disadvantage which imposed a severe restriction on the extent of its usefulness: at pressures in excess of 2 atmospheres (absolute), pure oxygen showed itself to be highly dangerous and poisonous in its effect if the breathing of it were prolonged. In effect, as is now fully recognized, the undiluted gas cannot safely be employed in an undersea operation at a pressure in excess of that encountered at 33 feet below the surface.

One answer to the problem is to have recourse to special breathing mixtures, tailored to suit the depth concerned— a highly specialized and involved technique about which more anon. Another, less complicated, and now widely adopted solution is to abandon the closed-circuit apparatus for an open type, designed to utilise ordinary air without any attempt at its regeneration.

III

The use of compressed air in a self-contained diving suit was advocated (though seemingly not attempted) in 1825 by William H. James. In this early design, the air, compressed to 30 atmospheres (450 pounds per square inch) was to be contained in a cylindrical belt, worn round the body of the diver over a waterproof tunic to which a copper (alternatively a leather) helmet was attached. From this head covering, a length of tubing led to the air container, the capacity of which was intended to allow an hour's submersion at a moderate depth (the exigencies of the situation are that the deeper a diver descends, the greater becomes his demand for air—*vide infra*).

Inspired, it is said, by an account of the William James proposals, two Frenchmen, Benoît Rouquayrol and Auguste

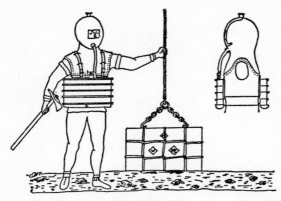

9. Self-contained diving suit based on the use of compressed air, as designed by William James in 1825.

Denayrouze, respectively a mining engineer and a naval officer, worked together from 1860 onwards to perfect a diving appliance which they termed an *aérophore*. In one of its several forms, it consisted of a close-fitting suit and hood of vulcanized rubber, fitted with a snout-like metal face mask which communicated with a drum of compressed air carried on the wearer's back. Normally, the air in the drum was maintained at a pressure not exceeding 30 atmospheres by way of a pipe-line from the surface, but if the need arose, the diver could detach the air-hose and so make himself independent of the external supply by relying on his stored air alone.

A unique feature of the suit was a novel regulating device, designed to provide the diver with air as he required it, while ensuring that the supply was maintained at a pressure which equalled that of the water at the level of his lungs. To this end, there was interposed between the helmet and the storage tank a conical valve, normally kept closed by the force of the imprisoned air, but which opened in response to the slightest pressure on its tail shaft. This shaft was in intimate contact with the rubber membrane of a compensation chamber, from which a feed tube extended to a mouthpiece, held by the diver between his teeth. Extreme sensitivity of operation was ensured by the fact that the surface area of the membrane in contact with the water was many times larger than the conical

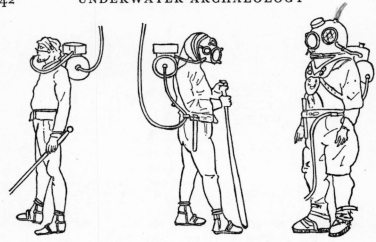

10. Three stages in the development of the so-called Áerophore *of Rouquayrol and Denayrouze, in which the diver is shown equipped with a nose-clip (left), a face mask (centre), and a helmet (right).*

head of the valve, so that a small drop in the air pressure of the compensation chamber relative to that exerted by the water surrounding it (a fall which could be occasioned not only by the diver inhaling, but also by his descending to a lower level) automatically depressed the membrane, causing the valve to open, thus admitting air until equilibrium was restored. Conversely, when the diver exhaled, or made his way towards the surface, his local air pressure exceeded that of the water about him, and the excess made its escape by forcing open the lips of a flutter (duck's beak) valve.

According to Dimitri Rebikoff,[116] an account to be found in an old French Navy manual describes how, as early as 1865, this equipment was safely used in underwater descents of 50 metres (164 feet), and its success was regarded as such that Jules Verne was moved to proclaim its wider possibilities when writing his well known *Twenty Thousand Leagues Under The Sea*. But although, with its ingenious air regulating device, the Rouquayrol–Denayrouze apparatus can rightly claim to be the true ancestor of the modern aqualung, in its day the inadequacy of metallurgical and other techniques severely limited its usefulness. Moreover, the diver was at first provided with little more in the way of extras than a nose clip, and in the absence of any form of eye protection, his vision was seriously impaired.* It was also found that during long submersions at depth, he suffered greatly from the cold, and in an attempt to overcome these difficulties, the aforementioned rubberized canvas suit with its snouted copper face mask was provided, complete with a viewing window, while in a still later version, a conventional style of helmet was adopted. In effect, one way and another, the outfit gradually became indistinguishable from Augustus Siebe's standard diving dress, the more so as the movements of the wearer were restricted to walking about the ocean floor, thanks to his possession of lead-soled boots. But an even more serious limitation was imposed by the want of a portable high pressure air storage tank, as this lack necessitated the use (at any rate for much of the time) of the customary surface pump and connecting air-line, thus throwing away the advantage offered by the revolutionary regulator, wherein the future of self-contained diving lay.

The next step was taken by Commander Yves Le Prieur, who had gained some experience of underwater activities while serving as a young officer in the French Navy. In 1925, at an exhibition in Paris, it chanced that some diving equipment attracted his attention. It had been devised a decade or so earlier (in 1912 or thereabouts) by Maurice Fernez, and consisted of a pair of detachable goggles, a nose clip, a weighted belt (fitted with a quick-release catch), and a U-shaped tube complete with a rubber nozzle, located centrally inside the bend. This mouthpiece was held between the user's teeth, the two arms of the U-tube extending over his shoulders. One arm terminated in a duck's beak valve, while the other led (by way of a length of hose attached to the belt) to an air-line with atmospheric connections, and down which a constant flow of air was pumped to the diver. After he had extracted as much of this as he needed, the excess escaped through the flutter valve,

*The omission is surprising, as the need to protect the eyes under water had long been recognized. Thus Ibn Battuta,[79] famous for his account of his travels throughout Africa and Asia during the fourteenth century, describes how Arab pearl divers resident in the Persian town of Quay, otherwise Síráf, were equipped with a nose clip and a tortoiseshell face mask. This last device would appear to date back to at least the second century A.D., on the evidence of a ceramic vase from Peru (now in New York's Museum of Natural History) which depicts a diver grasping two fish in his hands, and wearing a pair of goggles.

11. A diver wearing protective goggles, as depicted on a Peruvian vase of the second century A.D. (from a photograph).

carrying the exhalations of the user with it. The arrangement was one in which simplicity of operation vied with an excessive use of air, though this last was a feature of no great consequence, since the wearer remained tethered to the surface.

Le Prieur's interest, however, was in free diving, and in collaboration with Fernez, he set about converting the equipment. To this end, the air supply line was abolished and replaced by a cylinder containing air at a pressure of 150 atmospheres, which container was carried on the back in a harness. The modified apparatus was first tested in 1926, and subsequent trials led to the introduction of other important changes. Thus the discomfort occasioned by the wearing of goggles and nose clip, and the inconvenience of the mouthpiece, led to the replacement of these items by a mask which covered the entire face. And between this mask and the air container, Le Prieur interposed a Rouquayrol–Denayrouze type of demand valve, while as a precaution against infiltration, a spring-operated regulating device ensured that, whatever the prevailing air pressure inside the face covering, it was always slightly above that of the surrounding water. As a result, the tendency was for excess of air, together with the wearer's exhalations, to escape round the edge of the mask, rather than for any water to force its way in. Nor was this all, for when the new apparatus made its appearance in 1934, it incorporated a safety feature in the interest of the non-professional diver: the content of the compressed air cylinder (capacity 6·5 litres) was limited to 975 litres (under a pressure of $975/6·5 = 150$ atmospheres). This sufficed for a descent of 20 minutes duration at a depth of 7 metres (23 feet), or for one of 10 minutes at 12 metres (39 feet), this last the officially recommended limit if the hazards of decompression sickness were to be avoided without recourse to precautionary measures.*

The new and improved Le Prieur apparatus not only made the diver independent of the surface, but it transformed him from an upright walking to a free-swimming agent who was no longer restricted in his movements to stumbling about the sea-bed in lead-soled boots. Instead, freed at last from the dictates of gravity (since he now found himself in hydrostatic balance), the user was able to glide about at will in a three dimensional environment, in the manner of its piscatorial inhabitants.

The stage was thus set for the appearance of an even more advanced self-contained diving unit, embodying simplificative refinements which made it entirely automatic in action— *le scaphandre autonome* (the so-called 'autonomous diving suit', better known as the aqualung) associated with the name of Cousteau.

IV

Jacques-Yves Cousteau was born in 1910 at Saint-André-de-Cubzac, near Bordeaux, in Western France. Destined for a

*These capabilities were afterwards extended by Georges Commeinhes, whose modifications of the apparatus enabled him to attain a depth of more than 50 metres (164 feet) at Marseilles in 1943. To achieve this, diving time was appreciably increased by the use of a trio of 4-litre bottles, each containing air at a pressure of 150 atmospheres, whose combined capacity ($3 \times 4 \times 150 = 1,800$ litres) enabled nearly half an hour to be spent at 20 metres (65 feet).

12. Jacques-Yves Cousteau (from a photograph).

naval career, in 1936 he found himself posted to the cruiser *Suffren*, then based at Toulon. Here, he made the acquaintance of a fellow officer, Lieutenant Philippe Tailliez, with whom he shared an abiding interest in swimming and diving. It was while thus engaged, some two years later, that Tailliez was approached by Frédéric Dumas, another underwater enthusiast, and the three soon became inseparable companions, both in the sea and out of it.

Cousteau's own aquatic activities were of long standing, and dated back to a boyhood spent in Alsace. One day, after reading a story in which the hero eluded his pursuers by immersing himself in a river and drawing breath through a reed, he was inspired to emulate the exploit, though on a somewhat more ambitious scale. Intent upon carrying the strategem to what appeared to him to be its logical conclusion, he thrust one end of a garden hose through an improvised cork float and inserted the other end in his mouth. Then, carrying a heavy stone as ballast, he leaped into a swimming pool in the confident expectation that respiration would proceed as usual.

A graphic description of the inevitable and suffocative

outcome of such an action was subsequently published by Guy Gilpatric,[62] another hopeful attempter of the unachievable:

> Before you have gone either far or deep, you find that it takes a lot of muscular effort to drag the air down through the tube; you become conscious of the weight of water bearing in upon your chest and ribs; you feel yourself running out of air—so you cast loose your weights, shoot up to the surface, and charge it to experience.

This Gilpatric was an American writer who had made his home in Antibes, on the French Mediterranean coast. Here, in the course of practising his chosen vocation, he emerged as a leading exponent and advocate of skin (i.e., near naked) diving and spear fishing. In his own words, he became a 'goggler', a term derived from the one essential item of diving equipment which made undersea hunting possible: a pair of watertight spectacles. The weapons used ranged from arbalasts and spears to spring guns and powder-propelled arrows, and during the 1930s, so popular did the pastime become, that marine life in the coastal waters extending from Marseilles to Menton was threatened with extinction. The consternation and dismay of local fishermen may be imagined, and the sound of their protests, as they found their livelihood increasingly endangered, ultimately reached the ears of a not unsympathetic Government. The eventual outcome was the passing of legislation which had the effect of severely limiting the activities of the undersea marauders, who were required, among other things, to take out a hunting licence. Nor was this the only sequence to the affair, for an instinctive reaction on the part of some of the intended victims was subsequently observed. Thus Cousteau[34] has described how survivors among the larger deep-sea fish not only showed a tendency to keep away from the mammalian intruders whose presence they had hitherto ignored, but in keeping their distance they even displayed an ability (or so it seemed to the frustrated marksmen) to distinguish between short and long range weapons!

In addition to goggles, two other essential items of equipment came to be adopted by fish hunters—the foot fin and the snorkel tube. As in the case of eye protection (the necessity or which, as already noted, was recognized by Arab pearl divers of the fourteenth century), the idea of increasing underwater swimming efficiency by means of limb attachments is also far from new. Leonardo da Vinci long ago advocated the use of hand paddles for this purpose, as in later years did Giovanni Borelli and Benjamin Franklin,[57] both of whom also suggested the wearing of a similar device on the feet. Borelli's proposed foot fin, however, was intended to be of rigid construction, and when it eventually came to be tried out, it proved to be dangerous in use—not to the wearer, but to any other swimmers who happened to be within striking distance. In the event, it remained for Louis de Corlieu to develop (1926 onwards), patent (1933), and market (1935) the now familiar soft rubber flipper which has since come to be regarded as an indispensable aid to underwater movement. Apart from endowing a swimmer with fish-like agility, it also increases his motive power by almost half as much again, while at the same time relieving him of the need to use his arms in this connection, thus freeing his hands for carrying and other purposes.

As for the snorkel, the original deviser of this simple but effective respiratory aid is unknown. Gilpatric identifies one of its early users as Steve Butler, an English resident of Juan-les-Pins, whence knowledge of the innovation spread. At all events, when Frédéric Dumas, after watching Philippe Tailliez disporting himself in the water, afterwards introduced himself to the swimmer as he came ashore, he was surprised to observe, not only that the stranger's feet were encased in rubber fins, but also that he was possessed of a J-shaped tube, whose purpose was to enable him to fill his lungs with air whilst lying face downwards on the surface of the sea. It is also a matter of record that about the time of the Dumas–Tailliez encounter (which took place in the summer of 1938), Maxime Forjot, of Nice, incorporated such a breathing tube in an improved face mask for which he had obtained a patent the year before. But whatever its origin, and while it will be evident that the bent tube device represents no more than a specialized application of the age-old reed-in-mouth technique, in the days ahead the innovation was to prove a development of vital concern to underwater swimmers wearing self-contained diving apparatus. As experience was to show, it happened on occasion that an operator who chanced to surface far from a boat or the beach

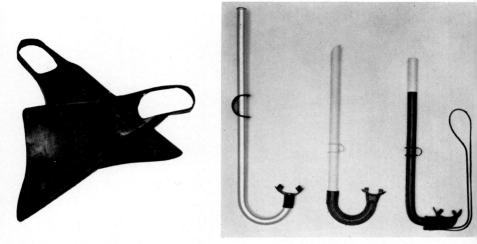

1. Black rubber swimfins. **2.** Snorkel tubes, made (left to right) of alloy, plastic, and rubber. (Photos: *Siebe Gorman*)

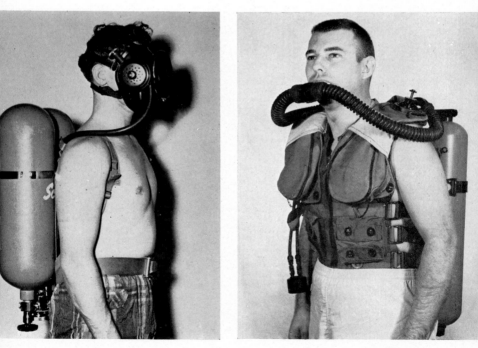

3, 4. Scott Hydro-pak self-contained underwater breathing apparatus. (Photos: *Scott Aviation*)

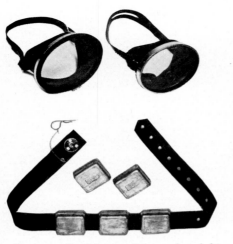

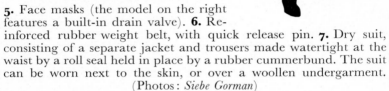

5. Face masks (the model on the right features a built-in drain valve). **6.** Reinforced rubber weight belt, with quick release pin. **7.** Dry suit, consisting of a separate jacket and trousers made watertight at the waist by a roll seal held in place by a rubber cummerbund. The suit can be worn next to the skin, or over a woollen undergarment. (Photos: *Siebe Gorman*)

8. Two-compartment decompression chamber, with accommodation for eight men (fourteen in an emergency). (Photo: *Siebe Gorman*)

found himself incapable of breathing while attempting to swim to safety because (1) the weight of the equipment on his back kept his face submerged; and (2) he was no longer able to draw upon his supply of stored air because it had all been used up. The value of a snorkel tube in an emergency such as this requires no emphasis, though it needs to be added that its value to an exhausted swimmer lying face downwards in the water is governed by the question of depth. Investigations (on the part of L. H. Lee Silverman and others) have shown that the centre of a user's chest should be not more than 3 inches below the surface, as beyond this level breathing becomes increasingly difficult and fatiguing.

The all-important contribution made by Cousteau and his associates to the progress of free diving, meanwhile, had its beginnings in a desire to prolong the length of their stay under water, not to mention the prospect of venturing to depths greater than the 60 feet or so to which they were restricted by their breath-holding capabilities—an ambition which called not merely for some form of diving aid, but for an aid whose performance was superior to that of any appliance then available.

For a year or more Cousteau gave his attention to the possibilities of a closed-circuit oxygen apparatus, which he himself designed and tested, only to convulse, with loss of consciousness, at a depth of 45 feet. A second such experience, during which, as a result of his once again blacking-out, he narrowly escaped death by drowning, convinced him that the oxygen-lung was as useless as it was dangerous for the purpose he had in mind. Without question, it seemed, the answer to the problem was to be found in the use of ordinary air, as employed (albeit somewhat extravagantly) in the systems devised by Fernez and Le Prieur. Of the two, the choice perforce lay with the apparatus of the last-named, since it was both self-contained and operationally the more efficient. It relied, however, upon a continuous flow of air, controlled by a hand valve, and what Cousteau visualized was the replacement of this arrangement by a mechanism which would automatically release air to the diver as and when he had need of it, thus conserving supplies and relieving the user of any responsibility in the matter.

In December, 1942, notwithstanding the restrictions on

4

movement imposed by the presence of enemy troops in his country, Cousteau travelled to Paris in search of an engineer likely to be able to assist him in his endeavour. He was thus brought into contact with Émile Gagnan, who showed his visitor a contrivance he had designed with a view to circumventing the prevailing fuel shortage by feeding cooking gas to automobile engines.

Some weeks of experimentation and adaptation followed, as a result of which there was devised a system in which control over a diver's air supply was exercised in two stages.* As a first step, the pressure of the contents of the storage cylinder was reduced from 150 atmospheres to 6, whereafter the air flowed to the user in the light of his requirements, with particular reference to the depth at which he happened to be (Rouquayrol–Denayrouze technique). Or such was the intention. But when the time came for Cousteau to test their handiwork in the waters of the River Marne, with Gagnan looking on, he made the disconcerting discovery that the instrument functioned as it was meant to do only when he assumed a horizontal position. If he stood upright in the water, he received an excess of air; conversely, a head downwards situation so reduced the flow that he was left gasping for breath.

What was wrong? During the return journey to Paris, the two reached the conclusion that the cause of the trouble was to be found in the vicinity of a special feature of the apparatus, a mouthpiece with combined intake and outlet tubes. Specifically, the fault was traced to the positioning of the used air exhaust in relation to the intake control, as the existing arrangement was such that the two items occupied the same level (and so became subject to the same external pressure) only when the diver lay horizontally in the water. If he raised his head above his feet (or *vice versa*), the balance between the inhalation and the expulsion of air was at once disturbed—an analysis in the light of which the solution to the problem seemed to be as obvious as it was simple: all that was necessary was to locate the escape valve alongside the demand regulator, an elementary but all-important consideration which forms the basis of the Cousteau–Gagnan patent.

*Subsequently (1955) replaced by a single stage operation in a new and advanced model of the aqualung, known as *Le Mistral*.

Unlike the Le Prieur appliance, the new apparatus did not include a pressure gauge, that the wearer might be kept informed of the state of his air supply. Instead, the cluster of two or three storage tanks, carried on the back in the conventional harness, incorporated a monitoring device which informed the diver when nine-tenths of his air had been used up. The arrangement was that when the cylinder pressure fell to 25 atmospheres, a spring-loaded valve shut off the supply. Thus warned, the diver then manipulated a reserve tap and promptly made his way to the surface.

Another characteristic feature of the appliance was that the wearer breathed (and exhaled) through a mouthpiece which was entirely separate from that part of the equipment which gave protection to the eyes. As a result, unlike the situation which prevailed when use was made of the full face mask favoured by Le Prieur, underwater telephonic communication was precluded. On the other hand, quite apart from the improved breathing arrangement, the method adopted offered certain advantages (among them safety in operation) when used in conjunction with a single pane viewing mask. As to this, the original Fernez goggles, with their cast aluminium rims and rubber surrounds, proved far from satisfactory in use, as the salt water quickly corroded the metal, while the cushioning obscured the wearer's view. Even when an improved version later appeared, replete with chromium plated fittings, a fundamental fault in design remained: unless the two lenses could be kept perfectly flat in relation to one another, i.e., maintained in the same plane, double vision underwater was the inevitable result.

Who first conceived the notion of solving this problem by substituting a single expanse of glass for the separate eye-pieces of the Fernez goggles remains a matter of conjecture. One name which has been mentioned in this connection is that of Alec Kramarenko, who devised such a piece of equipment, fitted with an air injection device intended to safeguard the wearer against the flattening effects of water pressure. But Kramarenko, it appears, copied the idea from the Japanese, who in turn, so Gilpatric relates on the authority of the person concerned, obtained it from Le Prieur. . . . In any event, the development did not end here, for the next step was to enlarge the visor so that in addition to the eyes, it also covered the nose, an organ evidently intended by nature to serve as a pressure equalizer. It was this improved form of the face mask, patented by Maxime Forjot in 1937, which Cousteau adopted for use with his air lung.

The crucial test of the improved apparatus, modified in the light of the River Marne experience, took place in June, 1943, in the vicinity of Bandol, on the French Riviera. Tailliez and Dumas were among those who stood by to provide assistance, should it be needed, as Cousteau, staggering under a 50 pound load, entered the sea. It was an anxious moment, but any feelings of apprehension were short-lived. The equipment functioned perfectly from the start, and continued to do so as it was subjected by its wearer to a succession of loops, somersaults, and barrel rolls: no matter what the position adopted, breathing went on normally and without conscious effort.

Cousteau's immediate reaction was one of cautious satisfaction. But several months and some 500 trouble-free dives later, after a series of exhaustive trials undertaken by all three members of the team, there no longer seemed any reason to doubt that a new and exciting age of undersea exploration was about to begin.

BERT

FLEUSS

HALDANE

Chapter Two

Difficulties and Dangers

I

With the means to make an extended stay under water at their disposal, the attention of free divers turned to the question of achieving deeper penetrations. Of possible concern here was the provision of sufficiency of air, as consumption of this vital commodity rose alarmingly with depth—twice the normal rate at 33 feet, three times at 66 feet, four times at 99 feet, and so on. Otherwise expressed, a portable tank which contained enough compressed air to sustain a diver for one hour at the surface would, at the depths listed above, suffice for $60/2 = 30$, $60/3 = 20$, and $60/4 = 15$ minutes respectively. Unless some means of increasing or supplementing a diver's supply of air could be found, descents to, and ascents from, lower and yet lower levels would inevitably take up a disproportionate amount of his total immersion time.

Then there was the matter of vision. The first essential, its restoration by protecting the eyes from direct contact with the water (as this was liable to cause irritation, and also resulted in an unacceptable loss of refraction power) had already been accomplished by means of the face mask. This piece of equipment necessarily interposed an air space between the water and the eyes, and as the two media have different refractive indices, some distortion of vision inevitably occurs, objects appearing

53

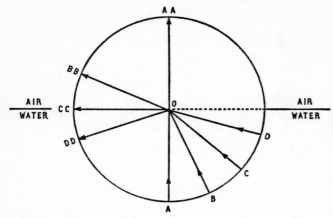

13. Deflection of light as it passes from one medium to another (e.g., from the water of the sea to the air space in a diver's face mask). The The change in density causes refraction of all but perpendicular light rays (those following the path A–AA), as illustrated by the line B–BB. Moreover, the angle of incidence (BOA) reaches a critical point when it attains a value of 49° (as at COA)—the emergent light ray then travels along the water surface (path C–CC). At angles greater than 49°, total reflection results (path D–DD).

to be larger and nearer to the viewer than they in fact are. But although divers at first found the phenomenon confusing, they soon learned to make allowances for it, as an alternative to wearing corrective spectacles (Dimitri Rebikoff system). Another minor problem, just as readily disposed of, was a tendency for the face-plate of the mask to mist over when in use, and chemists evolved special preparations, designed to obviate the trouble. But the simplest, cheapest, and most often used preventative proved to be the diver's own saliva, rubbed on the glass and then washed off. The name of the discoverer of this celebrated remedy has, alas, been lost to posterity, though a possible clue as to his nationality has been provided by Gilpatric:[62]

I met a Russian at Juan-les-Pins who had met a Norwegian at Villefranche who had met a Jap at Naples who said that at the Sakanaciuki school at Nagasaki, where a two-year course is given in goggle fishing, the pupils are taught to expectorate into their goggles as part of the ceremony of entering the water . . .

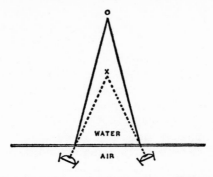

14. Refraction increases the angle of divergence of light rays as they pass from water to air, with the result that to a submerged and masked viewer, objects appear to be nearer than they actually are.

Be all this as it may, a diver's ability to see in his fluid surroundings is also governed by such considerations as turbidity and the hour of the day, not to mention the fact that absorption of the sun's rays by water increases rapidly with depth—to such an extent that at 50 feet down, the intensity of daylight is reduced to almost one tenth. This absorption, moreover, is highly selective, in that it is radiation at the long end of the solar spectrum which is the first to disappear from the scene. After 33 feet, there is no red; beyond 98 feet, no yellow; while at 165 feet, everything appears blue-green, whereafter a dim twilight prevails until total darkness is encountered at about 1,400 feet. The best that a diver can hope for is that at noon in clear water, good visability will extend for the first 100 feet of his descent, and that he will find himself able to see what he is about for another 150 feet. Thereafter, some form of artificial illumination soon becomes necessary.

More serious than the absence of light at depth was the promise of an accompanying lack of warmth. The extent of this problem naturally varies in accordance with geographic location and the time of year, though whatever the season, even the temperature of the favourably situated Mediterranean Sea remains disagreeably low as little as 50 feet down. And while icy waters may mean no more than a brief period of discomfort for a native diver dependent solely on the capacity of his lungs, even if his air supply were to permit it, he would find

himself unable to endure a prolonged stay in such chill surroundings. And while an obese person could expect to survive
longer than a thin one, the eventual outcome would be the
same: a progressive and catastrophic loss of bodily heat which,
if allowed to continue, would end in unconsciousness and death.

For deep penetrations, some form of protective clothing was
thus to be regarded as imperative, as Rouquayrol and
Denayrouze had acknowledged by adopting a waterproof
covering of rubberized canvas, reminiscent of the conventional
diving dress. As for this much maligned outfit, disdained by the
free diver because of its surface tether, its unwanted buoyancy
(not to mention its lead-soled boots), and its ungainly bulk, the
one great advantage it had to offer was that its loose-fitting,
air-filled suit both kept the occupant dry and permitted the
wearing of an ample thickness of clothing next to the skin. The
highly desirable result was that he remained warm and unwet
at all times, able (at any rate in so far as the question of temperature was concerned) to stay below for an indefinite period.

The lesson was not one that could be ignored,* and protective
suits developed for use by free divers (to whom, strictly, the
term 'skin diver' thereafter ceased to be applicable) can be
assigned to one or other of two categories—the wet and the dry.
As its name implies, the wet (also referred to as the free-flooding)
suit is not designed to keep the water out. Rather is its purpose
to diminish the rate of flow over the wearer's body, and so
reduce heat loss. In its earliest, most primitive guise, it merely
consisted of thick woollen underclothing, or even (as Honor
Frost[60] has revealed) a pair of ballet tights. To this makeshift
wardrobe, a dress made of sponge rubber in due course came
to be added, which remained in vogue until it was superseded
by the much superior and now widely adopted Neoprene foam
suit, replete with a hood attachment which covers the head and
incidentally affords protection to the nape of the neck, a vulnerable part of the human anatomy. Although the garment is
designed to fit the wearer closely, that it may not unduly hinder

*Especially as the age-old practice of rubbing the body with oil and grease had
been found wanting. The investigations of Cousteau and Company suggested that
once most of this covering had been washed away, the surface film which remained
merely served to increase the rate of heat loss. They opined, however, that if the
grease could somehow be injected beneath the skin, it would endow the recipient
with a blubber-like shield akin to that enjoyed by the whale!

his swimming movements, it allows a thin layer of water to come in contact with the skin, where the fluid absorbs bodily warmth and thereafter serves as an insulating medium.

Although the Neoprene wet suit has demonstrated its worth in connection with dives of moderate depth and duration, it becomes progressively less effective as a barrier against cold as the wearer descends. This is because its foamy substance becomes more and more compressed by the ever-increasing weight of water to which it is subjected—at 65 feet, the thickness of the material is halved, while after another 100 feet, it is reduced to one third. Moreover, in terms of heat loss, the effect is even more unfavourable than these figures might suggest, for whereas at 65 feet the leakage rate is doubled, at 165 feet it is found to have doubled yet again, by which time the flattened material has ceased to act as an efficient thermal insulator.

Where conditions of extreme cold have to be endured, the dry suit is much to be preferred. This waterproof garment is furnished with rubber seals at the neck and wrists, and is made sufficiently loose fitting for it to be worn over woollen clothing. But the fact that it is impervious to water introduces a problem. At the start of a dive, the suit necessarily contains a certain amount of air, the volume of which shrinks in response to external pressure, as a result of which the wearer is liable to suffer a severe bruising of his skin. At the same time, he may also experience a no less painful tendency for small folds of his flesh to become trapped and pinched by creases in the clothes he is wearing. However, these unpleasantries can be avoided. One answer, though it entails entering the water handicapped by an unwanted buoyancy, is first to provide the suit with an extra supply of air, calculated with reference to the intended depth of the dive. Another, and more satisfactory, solution is to inflate the suit while the descent is in progress, continuously adjusting the internal pressure to match that of the water, and it was from this idea that the so-called constant volume suit was evolved. In this last arrangement, instead of the additional air coming from a supplementary container, it is extracted from the breathing supply of the diver and introduced into the suit past the edges of an inner face mask which forms an integral part of the hood.

In the summer of 1947, the year following their development

of the constant volume suit, Cousteau and his team decided that the anticipated needs of the free diver in respect of warmth, vision, and air supply having been sufficiently met, the time had arrived for them to give their attention to the still un-answered question of depth: just how far down would the air-lung enable a man to go?

In a tentative exploration, earlier undertaken, Frédéric Dumas had descended to 62 metres (nearly 200 feet), and on surfacing had complained of hallucinary sensations, a phenome-non it was also proposed to investigate. The new target was set at 300 feet, and for those taking part, the procedure involved the marking of a series of white boards, attached to a weighted line at 5 metre intervals. Both Cousteau (who afterwards reported sharing Dumas' experience at 200 feet) and Tailliez (his acquisition was a massive, two-day headache) succeeded in reaching the last of the boards, whereupon further attempts were planned for the following autumn, with the target depth increased yet again. The first man to go down was Maurice Fargues, an experienced diver, and all seemed to be well until his periodic tugs on the marker line suddenly ceased. When he and the line were hauled to the surface, the markers indicated that a record depth of 396 feet had been reached. But Maurice Fargues was a drowned man, with his mouthpiece dangling uselessly on his chest.

From this tragic episode, two conclusions were drawn:

1. That the safe limit of free diving using compressed air lay somewhere between 300 and 400 feet; and

2. That beyond this limit, there existed a hazard which appeared to be a by-product of increased water pressure.

II

Liquids are but slightly compressible, and water is no exception: when 1,000 cubic feet of it are subjected to a pressure of 2 atmospheres, the reduction in volume which takes place is a mere 0·05 of a cubic foot. Even so, on an oceanic scale, the cumulative effect must be considerable, and it has been estimated (by P. G. Tait) that if the contents of the world's seas were suddenly to become totally incompressible, the aver-age rise in level would amount to 116 feet. However, for all practical purposes, the density of sea-water can be regarded as remaining constant at 64 pounds per cubic foot, and the pressure exerted as being directly proportional to the depth. Thus, at 33 feet down the weight of a column of water acting upon a surface area of 1 square foot will be $33 \times 64 = 2,112$ pounds, at twice this distance $2 \times 33 \times 64 = 4,224$ pounds, and so on. Be it further noted that 1 square foot $= 144$ square inches, and that $2,112/144 = 14 \cdot 7$ pounds per square inch $= 1$ atmosphere.

It follows that in the deepest parts of the ocean (over 36,000 feet) the pressure of water must exceed 1,000 atmospheres, the equivalent of some 7 tons per square inch. In the light of this information, biologists at once concluded that no marine life could possibly exist in the midst of such oppressive conditions, and this remained the accepted view until the record under-water descents of William Beebe, Auguste Piccard, and others proved by direct observation that living creatures did inhabit these dark and hitherto inaccessible regions.

How was this unexpected state of affairs to be explained? The answer, as it happened, had already been provided by the French physiologist Paul Bert,[11] when he disposed of the notion that ever-mounting water pressure would, of itself, quickly confront deep-sea divers with an obstacle which could not be looked upon as other than insuperable. Bert's investigations convinced him that water pressure, as such, offered no problem to fish or man, and that the anticipated crushing effects would take place only in circumstances where the walls of an enclosed, air-filled space were insufficiently strong to resist whatever forces they were called upon to bear. Thus a conventional naval submarine boat, because of the relative weakness of its hull structure, could not hope to escape destruction in the depths successfully attained by William Beebe and his successors in their specially designed pressure-resistant undersea vessels.*

As for the human anatomy, this consists almost entirely of

*It is of interest to note that the cast metal sphere in which William Beebe and Otis Barton, its designer, were lowered to depths of 2,000 feet and more in the 1930s, remained suspended at the end of a steel cable attached to a surface ship. This method of ensuring a safe return could not be used for the much deeper descents (over 35,000 feet) subsequently made by Auguste Piccard and his son Jacques. Instead, untethered craft were employed which relied for the ascent upon the release of ballast.

incompressible solids and fluids, and exhibits only a few cavities (lungs, sinuses, ears) which are liable to be affected by deep submersion. But if serious damage to these vulnerable areas is to be avoided, it is essential to ensure that the air within them is maintained at a pressure which matches that of the surrounding water, a requirement which has come to be appreciated only in comparatively recent times. Prior to this, stricken pearl seekers, echoing Aristotle,[3] could but enquire:

Why is it that the ear-drums of divers burst in the sea?

The answer to this question is to be found under the heading of aural barotrauma, a debility characterized by a functional failure on the part of the tube, named after the Italian physician Bartolommeo Eustachio, which serves to convey air into (or out of) the middle ear, thereby maintaining equality of pressure on both sides of the tympanic membrane. Usually, any difficulty attending this operation (which ordinarily occurs without conscious effort) is experienced when the external pressure is increasing rather than diminishing, i.e., when a diver is making a descent. Again, the Eustachian tube is normally no more than lightly closed, so that the simple and involuntary act of swallowing suffices to open it. But it may be found at the start of a dive that this is not the case, in which painful situation more positive action will be required, such as holding the nose whilst swallowing, or making rotatory movements of the jaw. If relief cannot be obtained by these or other means, then the dive should be abandoned, lest continued over-stretching of the eardrums result in perforation.

It might be thought that the deeper a diver goes, the more he will need to guard against such a contingency. But this is in fact not so, a seeming contradiction which is explicable in terms of the ubiquitous Gas Law of Robert Boyle:

Depth in feet	0	33	66	99	132	165	198	231	264 ...
Volume of air	1/1	1/2	1/3	1/4	1/5	1/6	1/7	1/8	1/9 ...

As will at once be seen, whereas a descent from 0 to 33 feet halves the volume, it requires an additional 66 (from 33 to 99) feet to reduce it to one quarter, and a further 132 (from 99 to 231) feet to halve it yet again. In other words, the rate of change progressively diminishes with depth, and with it the extent of some of the attendant hazards which an intruder has to face. Thus a suited diver who slipped off his surface stage into the sea, and sank for a distance of 33 feet, could suffer a severe squeeze as a result of his dress contracting about him when the volume of its air content was suddenly halved. But if a fall through a similar distance occurred at a depth of 594 feet, the air shrinkage would amount to a mere 5 per cent., and the risk of bruising would be negligible.

Of the various ills directly attributable to water pressure, the most serious is lung damage, the possibility of which (though for different reasons and in different ways) has to be faced by both equipped and naked divers. In his enquiry into the suscepti-bility of the last-named to this form of injury, S. Miles[96] bases his conclusions on an average lung capacity, when fully ex-panded, of 273 cubic inches, to which there needs to be added a residual 91 cubic inches. This gives a total lung volume of 364 cubic inches, from which it follows that at a depth where an absolute pressure of 4 atmospheres is encountered, the total volume will have been reduced to $364/4=91$ cubic inches=the residual volume. In short, a typical member of the breath-holding fraternity who descends to 99 feet will, without any loss of air, then find himself in a state of full expiration. A well defined (if individually variable) limit is thus imposed on the depth that is obtainable, even by the possessor of outsize lungs. And to attempt to venture far beyond it would be to invite disaster in the shape of pulmonary haemorrhage, cracked ribs, and a caved-in chest, as many an incautious victim has doubt-less learned to his cost in the past.*

The danger which confronts the aqualung user is the reverse of this, in that unless he takes the necessary precautions, he faces the prospect, not of implosion, but of explosion, with results no less calamitous. His situation is that he is able safely

*J. Y. Cousteau[34] records having witnessed a plunge to a depth of 130 feet, without the aid of breathing apparatus, on the part of a 60-year old Arab sponge gatherer. Even deeper (though non-working) penetrations have been claimed for Italian and Brazilian exponents, who seemingly reached a depth of 195 feet, while in 1967 Robert Croft is said to have established a record descent of 212 feet.

to attain depths far beyond the reach of the unequipped diver, and to remain there for an extended period of time, because he is being continuously supplied with air at the requisite (elevated) pressure. But when he starts his return to the surface, it is vital to ensure that air in this highly condensed state is not retained in the lungs, there to expand at an ever-growing rate as the weight of water bearing down upon him rapidly lessens. The mathematical implications of such a distension are truly alarming, as a consideration of an ascent begun at a depth of 231 feet serves to show. In the course of the upward journey, at

15. Arab sponge divers harvesting the Mediterranean (based on a contemporary engraving).

the 99 and 33 foot levels, the entrapped air will have doubled and then quadrupled in extent, while by the time the surface is reached, its volume will have increased eight-fold.

In aqualung diving, the condition referred to as burst lung (pulmonary barotrauma) is almost invariably the result of breath-holding during ascent, particularly when the victim is in the vicinity of the surface, where the relative pressure volume changes are greatest. And the effects can be as serious as they are dramatic. Like an over-stretched balloon, the lungs eventually rupture, producing tears in the surrounding tissue through which the escaping air may find its way into the pulmonary circulation in the form of bubbles. These tend to lodge in the arterial system, giving rise to air embolisms which have been known to interfere with the supply of blood to the heart and brain, causing death.

Treatment, and to be effective it must be applied instantly, consists of placing the patient in a recompression chamber and submitting him to air pressure, that the size of the offending bubbles may thereby be reduced and so enabled to make their way past the areas of obstruction. But if unnecessary fatalities are to be avoided, the only sensible course is prevention, especially as this calls for little more than a purposeful resisting of a natural inclination to hold one's breath under water. During an ascent, that is to say, the mouth should be kept open throughout the journey to the surface, thus allowing the expanding air freely to emerge in a prolonged, life-saving expiration.

III

In addition to direct physical (barotraumatic) effects, exposing the lungs to air at high pressure also gives rise to secondary complications. Of these incidental ailments, the unsuspected existence of one such hazard did not come to light until the 1930s, the nature and extent of another was first recognized about a century ago, while the history of a third is probably as old as deep-sea diving itself. The modern name for this last-mentioned affliction is decompression sickness, but in the past, its many victims have been accustomed to refer to it in terms of its various symptoms—the niggles, the bends, the staggers, the chokes. And although, in the medical parlance of today, these more picturesque and descriptive references have been grouped together under the more precise heading noted above, it can at least be claimed on behalf of the earlier nomenclature that it served to distinguish between mild and severe forms of attack, and also identified which part of the anatomy was directly concerned. Thus, in the niggles, as the name suggests, there is relatively minor discomfort, usually amounting to no more than an annoying ache, whereas the agony of the bends, often associated with the arms and legs, may reach such an intensity as to become unbearable. In a case of the staggers, identified, as might be expected, with an unsteady gait, it is the organ of balance that is affected, while in the no less aptly named chokes, characterized by cardio-vascular involvement, severe chest or abdominal pains are accompanied by an acute shortage of breath. This particular condition is also marked by shallow respiration, weakness of the pulse, and falling blood pressure—adverse tendencies which, if they remain unchecked, are likely to result in loss of consciousness and asphyxia.

Until the investigations of Paul Bert[11] (1833–86), the cause of decompression sickness remained hidden. For the professional diver, the malady represented an ever-present occupational risk which he was helpless to prevent or avoid. His work, that is to say, was undertaken in the knowledge that he might easily become permanently crippled, as the after-effects of one attack were aggravated by those of another. And yet it can hardly have escaped notice that trouble was more likely to be encountered after a long, as opposed to a short, period of immersion; or as the result of attempting a deep, rather than a short, descent; or (more pointedly still) when the victim had engaged in a succession of brief and relatively shallow dives, instead of making a single such plunge. Evidently, time and depth were of significance, in that each entailed increased exposure. But exposure to what? Not, it seemed, merely to water, if only because similar ills (collectively referred to as caisson disease) were experienced by workers on land who were concerned with tunnelling and allied activities, in which the maintenance of a high atmospheric pressure was often necessary to prevent flooding. It thus appeared that decompression sickness, in all its forms, was in some way associated with the inhalation of highly compressed air.

In Paul Bert's day, something of the behaviour of gases under pressure was known as a result of the studies made by the English chemists William Henry and John Dalton, who between them established (1) that the amount of gas which dissolves in a liquid at a given temperature is proportional to the pressure (Henry's Law); and (2) that when a mixture of gases is exposed to the action of a solvent, the amount of each gas that is dissolved is proportional to its partial pressure (Dalton's Law). Thus, if in the interest of simplicity, ordinary air be regarded as consisting of 79 per cent nitrogen and 21 per cent oxygen, it follows

9. Observation chamber, designed to maintain atmospheric pressure at depths of up to 200 feet. A battery of sealed-beam lights enables the occupant to search the area below him. **10.** Submersible decompression chamber. The diver enters at his working depth and is brought to the surface under pressure. The S.D.C. is then locked to a deck-mounted chamber, to which the diver transfers, there to undergo decompression procedure. (Photos: *Siebe Gorman*)

11. Decompression chamber and the S.D.C. mounted on a rail system, to ensure correct alignment when the two are locked together, prior to the transference of the diver while still under pressure. (Photo: *Siebe Gorman*)

12. (above). The Swedish warship *Vasa*—view of the lower gun deck, after excavation, looking towards the bow. **13.** (left). Lion mascaron decoration from one of the *Vasa*'s gun port lids. (Photos: *Maritime Museum and the warship* Vasa)

that the apportionment of the individual pressures which go to make up the 760 mm. of mercury (Latin *hydrargyrum* =Hg.) exerted by the mixture at sea level is 79 per cent of 760=600 mm. Hg. in respect of nitrogen, and 21 per cent of 760=160 mm. Hg. in the case of oxygen. These partial values relate to a total pressure of 1 atmosphere, and they would be doubled for 2 atmospheres, trebled for 3 atmospheres (equivalent to depths of 33 and 66 feet of sea water respectively), and so on.

Dalton's concept of partial pressure, in which each of two or more intermingled gases behaves as though it alone occupied the total volume of the mixture, has important implications in underwater respiration, as will later be seen. In the meantime, it was to be expected that, as the pressure of air in the lungs increased, so would the amount of its constituent gases which dissolved in the blood, though seemingly this was a fact of no immediate physiological consequence. And so it proved, for experience showed that trouble did not arise until after a diver had returned to the surface. As to this, when Paul Bert examined the blood vessels and tissues of animals which had been subjected to an equivalent sequence of events, he found that a return to normal pressure resulted in the release of innumerable gas bubbles, which came out of solution in the manner displayed by the contents of a bottle of soda water when the cap is removed.

This, then, was how decompression sickness was brought about, in that the bubbles followed the blood-stream of their host until they encountered an obstruction, where they lodged, so giving rise to one or more of the various manifestations of the malaise. Nor was this all, for it then transpired that the offending bubbles consisted almost entirely of nitrogen: the oxygen content of the air tended to be utilised by the body in the normal way as fast as it was released. As for the question of the immunity of the cetaceans, which air-breathing creatures were seemingly able to penetrate the depths of the ocean without difficulty, this continued to puzzle biologists and others until P. F. Scholander hit upon the answer. Thanks to the constantly replenished air supply of the human diver, the nitrogen content of his blood increases throughout the period of submersion, whereas the whale (apart from a reserve of oxygen stored in its

5

muscle tissue) has to rely solely on the air contained in its lungs.*

Once the cause of the illness had been ascertained, the remedy was apparent: immediate recompression, as in the case of air embolism. This treatment (and there is no other) has the effect of inducing the nitrogen to redissolve, so easing the pain. Thereafter, by way of a carefully controlled decompression, the gas can be permitted to pass from the tissues to the blood, and from the blood to the lungs, so making its escape at a rate which ensures its safe bodily elimination. But this, Bert insisted, was an operation which ought to be performed in the interest of prevention rather than in the expectation of a cure, particularly as all that was required was for the diver to submit himself to the process *while he was still in the water*. To this end, he should make a slow, steady, and long-drawn-out ascent, pausing at the half-way mark if need be, so that the formation of bubbles did not take place at a rate which was too fast for his metabolism to cope with the emergency. And although the procedure was tedious and time-consuming, at least it was preferable to experiencing the ills it was designed to prevent.

With the death of Bert in 1886, his work was continued by others, pre-eminent amongst whom was John Scott Haldane. One of the problems to which this distinguished physiologist gave his attention was that of finding a safe means of speeding the return to the surface of those engaged in deep-sea operations, that their working time might be extended and a fatiguing ascent ritual shortened. In this endeavour, he was assisted by the already established fact that, for all depths not exceeding 33 feet, i.e., involving pressures of up to 2 atmospheres absolute, a diver was immune to decompression sickness, no matter what the length of his stay under water. At all events, it was a knowledge of this observation which led to the making of a bold and far-reaching assumption, as Haldane[66] himself subsequently explained. He surmised that:

---

*Although members of the whale family, whose ancestors were land animals, are the most fish-like of the re-entrants, they are nevertheless creatures without gills and retain their lungs and other mammalian characteristics, including facilities (in the female) for the suckling of young. From this it follows, even though they spend the whole of their lives in the sea, that they cannot remain submerged for an indefinite period, and need to surface every hour or so. Ironically enough, a whale stranded on shore, notwithstanding that it is an air-breathing ex-land animal, will die of suffocation, its much-vaunted lungs crushed by the sheer weight of its outsize body.

The volume of nitrogen which would tend to be liberated is the same when the total pressure is halved, whether the pressure be high or low. Hence it seemed to me probable that it would be just as safe to diminish the pressure rapidly from four atmospheres to two, or from six atmospheres to three, as from two atmospheres to one. If this were the case, a system of 'stage' decompression would be possible and would enable the diver to get rid of the excess nitrogen through the lungs far more rapidly than if he came up at an even rate. The duration of exposure to high pressure could also be shortened very considerably, without shortening the period available for work on the bottom.

This reasoning, if correct, promised to transform the existing return procedure, for it would mean that a diver operating at a depth of 99 feet could make a relatively rapid ascent to 33 feet (thus halving the pressure) before he needed to halt on his way to the surface—a significant advance on the slow, uniform rate of ascent advocated by Bert.

In the years which followed, the worth of the Haldane theory was fully investigated and its validity established, at any rate in so far as the response of goats to simulated dives in a pressure chamber was concerned. Its author then prepared a set of decompression tables, in which the new ascent routine was calculated with reference to the duration of dives not exceeding the then maximum attainable depth (a limit imposed by the hand pumps of the day) of 210 feet. Official tests, subsequently undertaken on the Royal Navy's behalf in northern waters, were successfully carried out, whereupon the British Admiralty Diving Tables were introduced and quickly adopted by other maritime powers.* An important by-product of these investigations was a listing of the duration time of dives which could be safely made to progressively increasing depths without recourse to decompression halts on the return to the surface. This provided a set of time-depth values which, when depicted in the form of a graph, produced the so-called no-stop submersion curve for man.

An added complication was introduced by the question of multiple dives undertaken within a given period, because of the possibility that an excess of dissolved nitrogen might still be

*This was in 1906. An extension of the original tables, in which the depth was increased from 204 to 300 feet, appeared in 1933.

present in the bloodstream at the onset of any subsequent descent. A distinction thus needed to be made between a single and a repetitive dive, in which a single dive was the first dive of the day, calculated with reference to depth (i.e., the maximum attained) and duration (defined as the period of time which had elapsed from the moment of leaving the surface in descent to the start of the return journey). Any dive taking place within 12 hours of a previous underwater excursion was accordingly to be regarded as requiring special consideration in terms of decompressive measures.

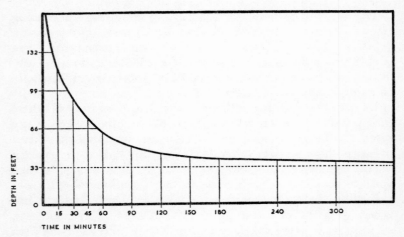

16. Graph depicting the no-stop submersion curve for man. For depths of 33 feet or less, no underwater decompression is necessary, no matter how long the duration of a dive.

Although the Haldane technique of decompression by stages represented a marked improvement on the method it replaced, it nevertheless entailed inconveniently long sojourns in the water if deep descents were involved. Thus a diver who went down 200 feet and remained there for an hour needed to spend more than twice this length of time in making his way to the surface, with no less than 8 stops on the way. And as, in the interest of those directly concerned, the Admiralty decreed that decompression time in the water should on no account exceed half an hour, this meant that working time at 200 feet was reduced from 60 minutes to a maximum of 10. Moreover, even an enforced stay of 30 minutes under water could prove exhausting to an already tired diver clinging to a guide line, and some means of making the experience less disagreeable was urgently required. One method which suggested itself was to furnish the diver with an air-filled, open-mouthed bell of the conventional kind into which he could clamber and seat himself, there to decompress as he was hauled up to the surface, his rope-suspended conveyance making the requisite number of stops on the way. The essentials of this operation were subsequently (1929) incorporated in a more elaborate piece of apparatus known as the Davis submerged decompression chamber (S.D.C.), consisting of a cylindrical steel vessel equipped with a telephone and able to accommodate two persons. The diver enters through a cover hatch (which is then closed), to find himself in a dry, well lit compartment and in the company of a resident attendant, trained to render any assistance he may need, including the administration of oxygen as a means of hastening nitrogen elimination. And unlike the ordinary diving bell, the decompression chamber, sealed off from the water by the closing of its hatch, can, in this airtight condition, be immediately hauled up to the surface and deposited onto the deck of the parent ship, where the occupants can be left to decompress in safety and in comparative comfort.

Even so, far too much of a diver's total immersion time continued to be taken up by his return to the surface, in relation to the period he was able to devote to doing useful work. And while the administration of pure oxygen (a procedure, incidentally, advocated by Paul Bert) materially helped to reduce decompression time, it was of strictly limited application because of the dangers which attend the breathing of that gas under pressure: in practice, for this reason, it is not used in the Davis submerged decompression chamber below a depth of 60 feet.

A fundamental difficulty associated with deep descents thus remained. But if the time required for making the subsequent ascent could not be further reduced, why not increase the length of the working session to such an extent as to bring about a reversal of the existing disproportion? In theory, this approach appeared promising, at any rate as a prospect (since realized*) of the future. For, irrespective of the depth attained, after a certain period of immersion, the amount of air dissolved in the blood and tissues reaches saturation point, beyond which the appropriate ascent (i.e., decompression) time remains static, no matter how prolonged the dive. Thus it appeared that an answer to the problem was to be found in an underwater habitation, giving access to the sea and replete with the necessities of life (air, food, water, warmth) in which it would be possible for a community of divers to reside more or less indefinitely.† For while it is true that (depending on the depth involved), on their eventual return to the surface they would face the prospect of several days of incarceration in a decompression chamber, they could in the meantime spend weeks or months usefully employed in the vicinity of their highly pressurized surroundings. However, before such a deep-sea colony could be established at depths in excess of 300 feet, yet another difficulty needed to be investigated and overcome: the evident unsuitability of ordinary air for use as a breathing mixture at pressures above 10 atmospheres.

IV

In 1930, with the assistance of motor driven air compressors, the British Admiralty began a series of deep sea diving trials. The aim was to seek to establish a safe working depth of 320 feet, and unusual behaviour on the part of those who approached this level was soon observed. Divers experienced a state of euphoria akin to alcoholic intoxication, accompanied

---

*In 1962, both Edwin Link and J. Y. Cousteau established inhabited undersea dwellings in Mediterranean waters, the former with his Man in Sea project (whose occupant remained at 200 feet for 26 hours), and the latter with his Conshelf I enterprise (in which men lived thirty feet down for seven days). These depths and times have since been considerably extended by various governmental undertakings, among them the U.S. Sealab and Tektite excursions, and the Kitzeh and other experiments conducted by the U.S.S.R.

†The idea of such an undersea community (though not one peopled by divers with open access to the ocean depths) was envisaged as early as the middle of the seventeenth century by John Wilkins,[146] later to become Bishop of Chester. Inspired by the submarine boat earlier invented by the Dutchman Cornelius Drebble, Wilkins wrote about the possibility of constructing a 'great Vessel' with 'lesser Cabins tyed about it' and went on to suggest that 'Several Colonies may thus inhabit, having their Children born and bred up without knowledge of land, who could not chuse but be amazed with strange conceits upon the discovery of this upper world . . .'

by a marked impairment of reasoning ability. The victim, however, remained blissfully unaware of what was happening. He tended, indeed, to become more and more confident as his capabilities decreased, and was given to performing extravagant and highly irrational acts, such as attempting to detach himself from his air supply, with the quixotic intention of rendering assistance to a passing fish, whose need for oxygen might possibly be greater than his own. Not infrequently, this feeling of contentment and camaraderie was followed by one of laziness and an almost irresistible desire for repose—Robert Stenuit[127] has described how he once found a diving companion, unmindful of an underwater assignment, stretched out on the floor of the sea, fast asleep!

Such incidents were both alarming and baffling, the more so as, on his return to the surface, the sufferer was often unaware that there had been anything amiss, and learned of some bizarre conduct or other on his part only because it had been witnessed by a fellow diver who happened to have retained full possession of his senses. It was thus to be counted a fortunate circumstance that individual susceptibilities appeared to differ widely, and equally gratifying that it was a common experience that as soon as a safe pressure level was reached, the symptoms disappeared completely without leaving any trace. There was no suggestion of a hang-over.

In an attempt to account for the phenomenon, it was ascribed in turn to increased oxygen consumption, to an excess of carbon dioxide, even to delayed claustrophobic effects. But in 1935, the American physiologist A. R. Behnke published the result of several years of research into the problem. According to the findings of his colleagues and himself, it was the nitrogen content of the atmosphere which was to be held accountable. Although this normally inactive gas had long been regarded as playing no part in respiration, other than to serve as an oxygen diluent, it appeared that when it was breathed under high pressure, it first produced excitation and then gave rise to a specific disorder which the investigators termed 'nitrogen narcosis'.

While this explanation gained wide acceptance, rival theories also continued to be advanced, e.g., that of J. W. Bean, who in 1950 attempted to revive the idea that carbon dioxide was the

responsible agent, a notion which C. Rashbass re-examined—
and found wanting—some five years later. However, it has
since been shown that other heavy (and normally inert) gases
can also produce narcosis when breathed under pressure, and
the probability seems to be that nitrogen (mainly) and carbon
dioxide (to a lesser extent) are both concerned, a recent suggestion being that they give rise to an anaesthetic effect by dis-
placing oxygen in the brain tissue.

Be this as it may, there can be no disputing the effects, or that
they become increasingly serious as a diver descends. Typical
symptoms, as catalogued in order of severity by S. Miles,[96]
range from light-headedness and over-confidence (100 to 150
feet) to hysteria and an indifference to personal safety (150
to 250 feet) leading to depression, muddled thinking, and
eventual unconsciousness (beyond 300 feet).* And it was clear
that this sequence of events offered a far greater threat to the
untethered aqualung user than it did to the helmeted diver, who
could always be hoisted to the surface by his attendants in an
emergency. As to this aspect of the problem, the French first
became aware of the danger in 1943, the year in which
Frédéric Dumas plunged to 62 metres (193 feet) and reported
finding himself the victim of strange imaginings. And it was
during a subsequent investigation, as already recounted, that
Maurice Fargues lost his life after descending to 396 feet, at
which point he seemingly decided to continue the dive without
benefit of air. Cousteau afterwards blamed the tragedy on
what he described as 'rapture of the depths' (*L'ivresse des
grandes profondeurs*), by which time there was general agreement
that for wearers of the self-contained air-lung, a depth of 300
feet represented the limit of human survival. Confirmation of
this was provided by the disappearance of the American
lawyer Root Hope who, despite all warnings, in December 1953
attempted a record-breaking descent from a boat equipped

*There is also some evidence to suggest that water pressure of itself can have an
adverse effect on the functioning of the higher nerve centres of the human brain,
in a manner not yet fully understood. According to investigations of the phenomenon undertaken on behalf of the U.S. Navy, the symptoms (which, as might be
expected, intensify with depth) take the form of a slowing down of the thought
processes, so that although a diver remains capable of following a set routine, he
finds himself at a loss if faced by an unexpected emergency. The dangers inherent
in such a situation need hardly be emphasized, though there are indications that
thanks to acclimatization, an experienced diver is less vulnerable than a novice.

with an echo-sounder. The graph produced by the instrument depicted the course of his journey into oblivion for the first 500 feet, whereafter all trace of him was lost. But even while he was still within range, he was undoubtedly unconscious, if not already dead.

Any possibility of a diver successfully making penetrations greater than 300 feet, it was evident, rested on his breathing something other than air, and the simple answer, it might have at one time been supposed, would be to eliminate the troublesome nitrogen and rely upon unadulterated oxygen. But as the investigations of Paul Bert had already shown, and users of the Henry Fleuss type of closed circuit breathing apparatus were to discover, exposure to pure oxygen under pressure promptly gives rise to convulsions and loss of consciousness. In view of this, modern underwater practice limits the employment of the pure gas to a working depth of a mere 25 feet, though the descent may be increased to 33 feet (involving a pressure of 2 atmospheres absolute) if no exertion on the part of the diver is required.

A strict observance of these precautions, however, does not entirely dispose of the problem of oxygen toxity. This remains a potential threat to a diver even when he is breathing ordinary air, though fortunately a critical situation does not arise until the depth limit imposed by nitrogen has been reached. Whereas at sea level the partial pressure exerted by the 21 per cent oxygen content of the air is 0.21 of an atmosphere, at a depth of 297 feet (the equivalent of 10 atmospheres) it becomes $10 \times 0.21 = 2.1$ atmospheres—slightly above the established danger point. Thus the surprising, not to say disconcerting, fact emerges that, beyond a depth of some 300 feet, a bar to further progress is offered by *both* the main constituents of ordinary air!

The approach to what at first sight might appear to be an insuperable problem is twofold, based on a limited retention of oxygen and the complete replacement of nitrogen. As the vital ingredient of any breathing mixture, oxygen clearly cannot be dispensed with in its entirety, but an essential proviso attending its use at depth is that at no time should its partial pressure be permitted to exceed 2 atmospheres. This, however, is a requirement which can be met only by means of a neutral diluent, so the problem becomes one of finding a nitrogen alternative which does not produce narcosis when breathed under stress. And in the search which followed, no more than two likely candidates were found, significantly the two lightest elementary substances known: hydrogen and helium.

The replacement of nitrogen by hydrogen in deep sea diving was pioneered during the mid-1940s by Arne Zetterström, a young Swedish engineer. A serious objection to its proposed use was its formation of an explosive mixture with oxygen when the two gases were present in certain proportions. However, in association with 24 parts of hydrogen, 1 part of oxygen was held to be safe, though such a combination could not sustain a diver at sea level. Accordingly, it became necessary to rely on other sources for the first 100 feet of the descent, at which juncture the increase in the partial pressure exerted by the oxygen content of the hydrogen mixture would suffice to make it breathable.

Having planned his dive in the light of these considerations, Zetterström began his descent breathing ordinary air, the oxygen of which, as a precautionary measure, he reduced to 4 per cent. immediately prior to transferring to the hydrogen mixture. This accomplished, he then made his way down to the record depth of 530 feet before signalling his readiness to be brought up. A number of decompression stops had been arranged for the return journey, but because of some misunderstanding, once the first of these had been made, he was immediately hauled to the surface, without pause even to change the composition of his breathing mixture at the crucial 100 foot level. Needless to add, he did not survive the experience.

With the death of Zetterström (duly certified as having been caused by a lack of oxygen and an acute attack of decompression sickness), divers confined their attention to the more promising possibilities of helium. The use of this non-inflammable gas as a nitrogen substitute had been proposed a quarter of a century earlier by the American physicist Elihu Thomson, since when a number of tests had been carried out in the U.S., Great Britain, and elsewhere. These culminated (in 1948) in a trial dive by William Bollard, R.N., who made a descent in the waters of a Scottish loch to a depth of 547 feet, and in so doing provided added confirmation of the suitability of oxy-helium: he remained mentally alert throughout.

Apart from the inconvenient fact that helium is a comparatively rare and costly substance, whose production has until recently been a U.S. Government monopoly, its use in diving operations is attended by a number of other complications. For one thing, the gas is exceptional as a conductor of heat, and accentuates the coldness of the depths to such an extent that the wearing of an electrically heated undersuit has been advocated. For another, it so distorts a diver's speech as to render it incomprehensible. And for a third, because of its highly diffusible nature and the somewhat involved process of bodily elimination to which this gives rise, stops deeper and longer than usual are required during the ascent to the surface, in accordance with a specially compiled set of Decompression Tables.

These difficulties, however, may be regarded as of secondary importance. The essential point is that artificial atmospheres are now available for use by divers which will give access to submerged areas hitherto (and otherwise) far beyond reach, as the recent underwater exploits of the Swiss Hannes Keller have served to show. With his descent to 1,000 feet off the coast of California in 1962, he demonstrated that a vast and previously inaccessible region of the earth's surface is now within man's reach.

V

The limit of undersea penetration with the aid of artificial atmospheres has yet to be determined, and in the meantime another and still more radical approach to the problem has been advocated : the breathing of water by humans, instead of a gaseous mixture. Experiments with mice have shown that these creatures can be kept alive, totally submerged, for hours at a time (and dogs also, though for a shorter period) in water which has been extensively enriched with oxygen. In such favourable circumstances, trials have indicated that the lungs of mammals can function in much the same way as the gills of fish, and Russian scientists foresee the day when mankind will be enabled to live and work on localized areas of the sea-bed by such means, untroubled by the need to wear any form of breathing apparatus. Nor is this all. J. Y. Cousteau has carried this line of thought a stage further. He envisages the surgical manipulation of healthy adolescents so as to produce a species of manfish,

17. The giant squid, which can attain a length (including tentacles) of 60 feet or more, is the largest of the invertebrates. Eighteenth-century seafarers credited the creature with ship-demolishing capabilities, as this engraving of the period shows (after Buffon).

endowed with artificial gills, whose lungs have been rendered inoperative by filling them with an incompressible fluid. Thus created, it is claimed, *Homo Aquaticus* would be enabled to descend to depths measured in thousands of feet, undeterred by any prospect of his experiencing decompression sickness or nitrogen narcosis.

One hazard would nevertheless remain: the possibility of a display of hostility towards the latest re-entrants on the part of some members of the resident population. Experienced divers, however, are unanimous in dismissing as minimal or non-existent any danger of attack from barracudas (held to be harmless), sting rays (which strike only if molested), giant mantas (devoid of any aggressive inclinations) and octopi (completely inoffensive, though the outsize squid, whose haunt is the ocean depths, is perhaps another matter). As for the much maligned shark, more than 300 different kinds are known, most of which display not the slightest inclination to attack man, and the consensus of informed opinion is that even the score or so species which do not belong to this category seldom cause trouble. On the other hand, there can be no denying that sharks have been the cause of not a few fatalities, especially in Australian waters, and some swimmers resort to a chemical substance (cupric acetate) which, when dissolved in water, is held to act as a repellant. And more recently, for the benefit of flyers who are forced down in the sea, the U.S. Navy is reported to have developed a battery-powered hand weapon which can fire a dart with sufficient force to halt any would-be attacker in its tracks.

Of more serious concern to divers, it would appear, are such comparatively lowly life forms as fire coral, sea poison ivy, jelly fish, and the sea urchin. Of these, the first three can inflict stings of varying severity, those of the dreaded colonial hydroid *Physalia Physalis* (Portugese man-o'-war) on occasion proving fatal. For its part, the sea urchin bristles with needle-like spines which, when trodden upon, penetrate the flesh of the victim and break off, causing exceedingly painful wounds which are liable to become infected and, by so doing, may also lead to death. Finally, there is the killer so-called whale (*Orcinus orca*), which is actually the largest representative of the dolphins. Like all members of the cetacea family, the killer is carnivorous, and fully lives up to its name. Endowed with a high degree of intelligence, it hunts its prey co-operatively in packs, displaying in the process a speed and ferocity which unquestionably make it the most dangerous of all known aquatic animals. As Owen Lee[91] has said:

There is no treatment for being eaten by the *orca* except reincarnation.

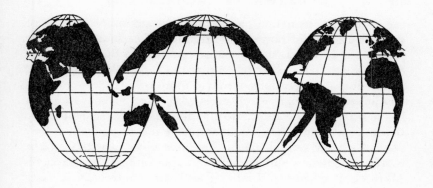

Chapter Three

Some Aspects of
Underwater Archaeology

I

In as much as the task of archaeology is the investigation of the material remains of past human activity, it is understandable that its practitioners began by confining their attention almost exclusively to dry land—the natural habitat of mankind. Moreover, even when restricted in this manner, the scope of the enterprise remained so vast in terms of time (a million or more years) and place (a region of some fifty-seven million square miles) that it promised to keep all concerned fully occupied for many decades to come. Any idea, meanwhile, of increasing this area of search by an additional 139 million square miles, the whole of which was permanently, and much of it deeply, covered by water, was clearly not a notion seriously to be entertained. Quite apart from its evident impracticability, what was there to be gained from an exercise which held out promise (so it was argued) of little more than the recovery of objects more easily to be found elsewhere—unimpaired by centuries of immersion?

This attitude towards the possibilities and prospects of underwater archaeology continued to be maintained until comparatively recent times (there are rigorists who cling to it still) with the result that, by default, a new and exciting sphere of interest was left almost entirely to the attention of persons outside the profession. In effect, there was a repetition of the sequence of events which had earlier taken place in the Valley of the Nile, where untold generations of native tomb robbers were eventually joined by foreign adventurers who, after flocking to Egypt in the wake of the Napoleonic invasion, then proceeded to strip that ancient kingdom of all the movable relics upon which they could lay their vandal hands. The next phase was that of the more enlightened entrepeneur, as personified by François Mariette, but whose official and well meant intervention, once he had been placed in charge of the newly established Service of Antiquities in 1858, did little, alas, to improve the existing situation—he merely decreed (to paraphrase the discerning James Baikie[5]) that, henceforth, the only plunderer should be himself. Thus, one way and another throughout the greater part of the nineteenth century, pharaonic treasures beyond reckoning were looted and sold, mishandled and despoiled, scattered and lost.

At the time, of course, archaeology was still in its infancy, and its early exponents can hardly be blamed for their failure to practice the niceties of a scientific method of investigation which had yet to be devised. But although, in the years which followed, much needed experience was gained, and expertise developed, in respect of sites in Egypt and other countries, few attempts were made to evolve techniques suited to an aqueous environment. As for archaeologists acquiring a practical knowledge of diving, doubtless the mere prospect of this provided learned academicians with yet another sound reason for limiting their field activities to dry land, in which decision, it may be supposed, their possibly more enthusiastic disciples were adversely influenced by the disinclinations of their elders. . . .

However this may be, at the start of the present century reliable (if somewhat cumbersome) underwater equipment was available for those who chose to make use of it, prominent amongst whom were sponge gatherers and salvage operators. Members of the learned professions (with one honourable exception—the French naturalist Henri Milne-Edwards) were inexcusably slow to take advantage of the opportunities thus offered, with the result that it was left to those who made deep diving their livelihood to stumble upon mounds of what proved to be historic debris, lying untouched upon the floor of the sea. But although considerable archaeological interest was aroused by such episodes, little in the way of an *in situ* examination, still less of a methodical and recorded excavation, was attempted, or even seriously contemplated, if only because there was an almost complete lack of trained personnel capable of undertaking such a task. All that could be done was to engage the services of the original finders, that they might extend the area of search and bring up any additional items they happened upon—a far from satisfactory arrangement which, perforce, became the accepted procedure.

The outlook for the future, however, was not quite so bleak as this unedifying situation might suggest. During the same period (i.e., from 1900 onwards), as will in due course be recounted, the pioneer activities of underwater investigators such as R. T. Gunther, Gaston Jondet, and Antione Poidebard, though their efforts admittedly concerned relatively shallow waters, served to draw attention to the possible workableness of submerged sites, given their accessibility. As to this, just as the area of search on land was greatly reduced by climatic and geographic considerations (in as much as the remains of ancient centres of population were more likely to be found in fertile river valleys, rather than in the midst of inhospitable deserts*), so the extent of archaeological operations under water was limited by the question of depth. In effect, the project assumed much more manageable proportions with the realization that, at any rate for the time being, it was likely to be restricted to the 11,000,000 square miles of the continental shelf.

II

At this point, it is instructive to enquire how it happens that things made and used by man come to be under water at all, and a moment's reflection suffices to show that there can be but two possible explanations. Either:

(1) The items in question were originally situated on land

---

*Though it has always to be remembered that in the past waterways have on occasion changed course, and that on some of the barren wastelands of today, trees and other greenery may once have flourished.

6

which subsequently became flooded because of (a) subsidence; or (b) rising water levels; or   (2) The said items were (a) deliberately submerged (harbour foundations; block ships; sacrificial offerings); or (b) accidentally lost (e.g., by shipwreck).

From this analysis, an interesting fact emerges in respect of the long established archaeological approach to the activities of mankind on the basis of whether they took place before, or after, the appearance of written records. With the exception of the sudden inundation of land brought about by tectonic movement (e.g., an earthquake, an occurrence which is liable to happen at any time) the causes listed under category (1) above belong to the Prehistoric Period (since the last post-glacial rise in sea level subsided before the invention of writing), whereas those shown under category (2) may be assigned to the Historic Period (if only because they relate to a degree of attainment commensurate with a knowledge of how to represent speech in the absence of a speaker).

But even on land, the Prehistoric Period (and this despite its inordinate length of a million or more years) has provided relatively scant evidence of human handiwork, apart from numerous cave drawings and a plentiful supply of Stone Age implements. And while it is true that Palaeolithic Man was free to roam over vast tracts of low lying territory which are now covered by the sea, there is no reason to suppose that an archaeological interest in these flooded regions would produce anything that was startingly new in the way of flint knives, arrowheads, and the like, though to the typologist all such finds are of significance. Thus a crustal disturbance which brought about the submergence of forest land at Leasowe, in the Wirral peninsula (as evidenced, at low tide, by the existence of extensive peat beds, interspersed with tree stumps) has been associated with a like movement in the Mounts Bay area of Penzance, where the discovery of the site of a now water-covered stone axe factory enabled the date of the subsidence to be placed somewhere between 1800 and 1500 B.C.

Similarly, the recovery (during dredging operations) of a Maglesmosian bone harpoon, 25 miles off the coast of Norfolk, points to the existence of a land bridge between England and Denmark in Mesolithic times, a conclusion chronologically in

18. The British Isles as part of the European mainland during the Ice Age, as suggested by the present 30 fathom line (after R. H. Davis).

accord with evidence derived from other sources. For although the chalk ridge which once joined Dover to Calais was almost certainly breached by melt-water during the Mindell–Riss Interglacial Period (580,000 to 430,000 B.C.), the connection was re-established in the course of subsequent glaciations, and was not permanently severed until after the ending of the last of these occurrences. According to F. E. Zeuner,[152] the probability is that the final separation took place sometime between 7000 and 6000 B.C.

As a result of what has been described (by G. Dubois) as this Flandrian transgression, throughout which, thanks to the melting of the last ice sheet, there was a gradual rise in sea level of some 400 feet,* doubtless various cultural links with our remote forebears were engulfed by the waters of what is now the English Channel. But it would be over-sanguine to suppose that much in the way of this evidence still remains to be found, while the fortuitous manner in which the Maglesmosian missile was reclaimed from the depths, emphasizes the difficulties which would attend any purposeful attempts at recovery.

The situation in respect of the Historic Period, on the other hand, appears much more promising. In Western Asia, the invention of writing occurred about the time of the discovery of how to smelt metal, and both these far-reaching events were accompanied by (and assisted in) the rise of early civilizations among the inhabitants of Mesopotamia and Egypt. Intellectual accomplishments apart, a characteristic feature of the achievements of these first city dwellers was the development of a monumental architecture (based on the use of brick or stone) and a plentiful production of household and other goods. In effect, the rise (and subsequent decline) of these urban communities have provided modern investigators with a series of unprecedented accumulations of archaeological material, by no means all of which has since awaited a finder on land. For in the past, not only have entire coastal settlements been known to slide bodily into the sea as a result of some localized geologic upheaval, but their now mud covered whereabouts are on occasion well attested, thanks to references contained in official records and eye-witness accounts.

But although not a few of these sites are known, an exploratory visitation has invariably convinced members of the search party that the making of a detailed examination, involving excavation, would be a task of such magnitude as to place it, if not beyond present-day capabilities, then at any rate outside the limit of any available finance. So for the time being at least, such an undertaking cannot be regarded as other than a possibility of the future, and attention has accordingly turned to less ambitious projects of more immediate interest. And while,

---

*Offset, to some extent, by a compensatory uplift of land masses (isostatic re-elevation) as they were relieved of the immense weight of their frozen burden.

in general, these include individual artifacts and relatively minor structural remains (such as ancient harbour works), in particular they concern members of that vast company of sunken ships which, from one cause or another, have found a last resting place beneath the waves since the first sea-going vessels began making their epic voyages of exploration and discovery.

There are a number of reasons for engaging in this last-mentioned study. Apart from sundry items of information contained in the writings of contemporaries, and the (not always accurate*) artists' impressions to be found on vases and

19. Mycenaean representation of a ship, as depicted on a vase from Cyprus (after E. Sjöqvist.)

elsewhere, little enough is known about the size, carrying capacity, and mode of construction of the ships of antiquity—even the precise manner in which the triple banks of rowers were seated in a galley such as the trireme has long been in dispute. And there would seem to be small prospect of our ever obtaining the answers to some of these questions on land, notwithstanding the occasional finding of well preserved specimens of boats in underground locations. Such vessels were usually intended to serve a symbolic purpose, as is evident from the ship burial disinterred at Sutton Hoo in 1939, and the still more recently discovered (1954) boat graves associated with the Great Pyramid of the fourth dynasty Pharaoh Kheuf.

*Thus a painting on an Attic cup by the potter Exekias, depicting an Athenian penteconter of the sixth century B.C., shows only 22, instead of 25, of the vessel's 50 oars.

Although the early history of floating craft (by way of logs, rafts, dugouts, and inflated animal skins) remains a matter of speculation, the Gerzeans of Egypt (who reached that land from Asia, c. 3500 B.C.) commemorated a notable advance by decorating their pottery with pictures of multi-oared vessels with twin cabins—held to be the earliest known representation of boats made from planks. These novel craft were subsequently fitted with sails, an addition inspired, no doubt, by an appreciation of the fact that the Nile River flows in a direction the opposite to that of the prevailing wind. Thereafter, as the records show, military and trading expeditions were despatched to far away places, among them the long unidentified Land of Punt (Puoni), famed for its gold, its ivory, and its frankincense —a destination which has since been named, with some degree of probability, as Somaliland.

However, it was not the Red Sea, or even the Indian Ocean beyond it, which was destined to become the cradle of navigation, but the more readily accessible Mediterranean, into which the waters of the Nile itself flowed. This longest of all rivers not only ensured Egypt's crops (by its annual flooding, which regularly brought down fresh supplies of fertile mud), but it also constituted the country's main highway to the sea, a sea unique in that it took the form of an almost tideless lake enclosed by the shores of three continents—the veritable centre of the known world. Small wonder, in these exceptional geographic circumstances, that this island-dotted expanse of water was fated to become the birthplace of sea-borne commerce, for it provided the shortest (and often the only feasible) means of communication between the many and diverse peoples of Africa, Asia, and Europe.

III

The Mediterranean Sea is the relic of a much more extensive body of water known to geologists as the Tethys (or Midworld) Sea, a great trough-like ocean which in Mesozoic times extended across the Atlantic from Mexico to Indonesia and beyond. Extensive earth movements subsequently brought about the uplifting of parts of the floor area, producing vast mountain chains (Alps, Pyrenees, Himalayas), in the course of which a land-locked depression was formed, containing a number of lakes whose borders served to link Spain (*via* Gibraltar) and Italy (by way of Sicily) to Africa.

The Straits of Gibraltar are believed to have come into existence shortly before the onset of the Ice Age, and the sill over which the waters of the Atlantic continue to pour (thanks to a permanent difference in level occasioned by evaporation) rises in at least three places to within almost 1,000 feet of the surface. The flooding of the region, which assumed its present outline as a result of the Flandrian transgression, drowned the land connection which extended from Sicily to Tunisia, converting it into the Adventure Bank. This submarine ridge now divides the Mediterranean into western and eastern regions, each containing a trio of (erstwhile lake) basins where the depth of water may exceed 15,000 feet. Even so, the extent of the sea-bed that is accessible to divers remains forbiddingly large, and it is only in recent years that various considerations have combined, substantially to reduce the element of chance which must inevitably attend the making of an organized search for the remains of sunken ships.

It may be accepted, for example, that once the early voyages of exploration had been undertaken, and commercial contacts between various peoples established, fairly well defined lines of communication would then develop, extending back and forth between recognized departure and arrival points. Seemingly, the process began when the Egyptians undertook a tentative investigation of the coastal regions in the vicinity of the mouth of the Nile. At all events, by sailing eastwards from the Delta, they eventually reached the heavily timbered land of the Lebanon, to which destination, in the year 2700 B.C. or thereabouts (so an inscription on a fifth dynasty stele informs us) the Pharaoh Snefru despatched an expedition of 40 ships to collect a cargo of cedar wood. After this, a regular exchange of goods took place between Egypt and what was known as the port of Kupna (later to be called Gubla by the then resident Phoenicians, and Byblos by visiting Greeks—the modern Jebeil).

In the centuries which followed, as Egyptian power and influence ultimately began to wane, other maritime peoples successively gained prominence, notably the Cretans (whose authority in the Aegean and elsewhere was maintained by means of strong naval forces); the Phoenicians (renowned for their widespread trading activities, and for the number of ports they established); the Greeks (whose aggressive inclinations not only led to bitter internecine strife, but also brought them into conflict with Cretans, Etruscans, Carthaginians, and Persians alike); and the Romans (the first people in history to dominate the entire coastline of the region), by which time sea-going vessels had come to be classified according to whether they were designed for purposes of war, for the speedy transportation of passengers, or for the carrying of cargo. And it goes without saying that any sunken examples of the last-named promised to be of particular archaeological interest, in that freight of all descriptions must have been conveyed across the Mediterranean from 3000 B.C. onwards—and have suffered many a shipwreck in the process.

Such investigations as have already been carried out suggest that while much of the early seaborne merchandise comprised raw materials and finished products (as exemplified by such items as copper ingots and pottery ware), it was more likely than not to consist of consignments of food and drink contained in amphorae. At all events, throughout the period from the fourth century B.C. to the sixth century A.D., these ubiquitous storage jars—'the jerrycans of antiquity', in the words of James Dugan[48]—were in general use for the conveyance of a wide variety of potable and edible commodities, which ranged from wine and olive oil to nuts and salted fish (*garum*). But that on occasion cargoes of a less mundane nature were also carried is known from the works of writers such as Cicero and Petronius, with their pointed references to the ostentation of those Romans, from the Emperor down, who collected foreign art treasures with which to adorn their palaces and villas. Many of these priceless (and often not so priceless*) marble and bronze

---

*Such was the insatiable demand for Greek works of art among Rome's leading citizens that it greatly exceeded the supply, and the need was met by an army of copyists, prominent amongst whom was a certain Pasiteles. A master of mass production techniques, he has been credited with the devising of an ingenious pointing machine, and with the perfecting of a much used moulding process. At all events, by one means or another, thousands of items of this duplicated art were produced, not a few of which still exist, fragmentarily or otherwise, to provide us with a tantalizing glimpse, if only at second hand, of examples of the superb workmanship of Myron, Phidias, Praxiteles, and the rest.

acquisitions, which somehow managed to survive until as late as the Middle Ages, were burned for lime during this period, or melted down for their metal content. But even if, on land, this wanton destruction of (predominantly) Greek art was all but complete, is it not possible that some of the purloined items were loaded onto ships which failed to reach their intended destination? By an ironic twist of fate, that is to say, might not the originals of some of the stolen masterpieces have been saved for the benefit of a more appreciative posterity by their being lost at sea?

An answer to this momentous question was first provided in 1900, by a team of sponge divers operating near the small island of Antikythera, when these *sphoungarades* chanced upon the wreck of a Roman argosy, heavily laden with a wealth of statuary, apparently looted from the temples and sanctuaries of Ancient Greece! This and subsequent finds provided magnificent examples of what were considered to be the original works of master sculptors belonging to the Argive and Athenian Schools in the fifth century B.C.—remarkable and exciting discoveries, made long before the aqualung appeared on the scene, which induced Salomon Reinarch, a leading Hellenist, wistfully to declare (*Gazette des Beaux-Arts*, II, 1928):

> The richest museum of antiquities in the world is still inaccessible to us. It lies at the bottom of the eastern Mediterranean. We are able to explore the land and the air without much difficulty, but we are very far from rivalling the fish in their element, who, in the words of Saint Augustus, have their being in the secret ways of the abyss. Those ways remain closed to us.

IV

Reinarch's remarks were made in anticipation of the day 'when the progress of science will permit us to engage in that exploration', and now that this day has dawned, investigators are faced by the task of locating and retrieving some of the widely scattered accumulations of archaeological material which bestrew the sea-bed. As a first step, many (if not most, or even all) of the ancient harbour towns of importance have now been identified, that of the long-lost Ras Shamrah-Ugarit as recently as 1929. The knowledge of the precise whereabouts of these ports, and of the nature of the trading activities associated with them, has led to the tracing of many of the old sea lanes, though a distinction needs to be made between sea crossings which entailed passing directly over the central deeps, and coastal journeys which did not. Happily, thanks to the navigational shortcomings of the times, early mariners showed a marked preference for sailing during the day and for remaining in sight of land, and seemingly liked nothing better than to find themselves in the vicinity of a rugged coastline which enabled them to steer a course from one headland to the next. Such journeyings, moreover, were usually made with the aid of *peripli*, descriptive narratives applicable to a particular route, complete with sailing directions. Informatively enough, a number of these detailed instructions have survived, one or two of them, e.g., those of the Carthaginian Hanno (giving details of a journey southwards from Gibraltar along the West Coast of Africa) and of Scylax of Caryanda (relating to coasts throughout the Mediterranean) dating as far back as the fifth century B.C.

This predilection for offshore voyaging is to be regarded as doubly fortunate from an archaeological point of view. Not only did it ensure that if a ship capsized and sank, it did so in relatively shallow waters, but it also added to the risks of the journey and so increased the possibility of its ending in disaster. For one thing, busy shipping lanes inevitably attracted the attention of pirates (who infested the Aegean, according to

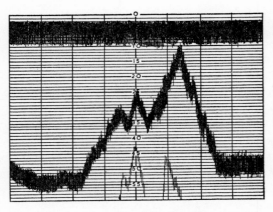

20. Typical sec outline, as traced by echo-sounding apparatus.

Thucydides,[137] as early as 1500 B.C.), and for another, many of these routes were also the scene of innumerable clashes between rival naval forces, as history records. Again, in the neighbourhood of promontories (such as the notorious Cape Malea) and narrow straits (e.g., those of Messina), gusting winds and treacherous currents were frequently to be encountered, and both were a source of trouble to the unwieldy sailing craft of the day. But perhaps the greatest threat to coastal traffic came from what the French call *secs* (the *secci* of the Italians)—pinnacles of jagged rock which rise, unseen, from the sea floor to within a few feet of the surface, ready and waiting to tear open the underside of any ship which attempted to pass over them. And finally, to these and other hazards there needs to be added the ever-present dangers associated with sudden storms and bad or indifferent seamanship, not to mention a high incidence of gross overloading. So it may well be that in the days of Classical antiquity, as Jean Rivoire[87] maintains, the total number of vessels lost in the Mediterranean must have amounted to many thousands.

Evidently the place to seek members of this sunken multitude is not merely within the confines of established shipping lanes, but at particular places along them, a pinpointing procedure successfully adopted by Cousteau[33] and his companions during a reconnaisance made in 1953:

> To find Aegean wrecks we followed the old trade routes. Any reef or cape that looked treacherous to us may have been fatal to the ancients, so we dived there. At every spot we found the litter of an old ship and, on several, signs of two or more . . .

On the other hand, searches for the remains of warships in vicinities where naval battles are known to have been fought have been less rewarding, in that, to date, none has been found. Various explanations have been offered to account for this disappointing outcome. Honor Frost[60] makes the point that since fighting craft were propelled by oars, they would be independent of winds which might bring disaster to a ship that relied entirely upon sails. And she adds that even if sinking took place, a naval vessel which kept its decks cleared for action would rapidly become covered by silt. Conversely, it has been argued (by N. C. Flemming[43]) that because of their comparatively

light tonnage, and even after they had been extensively
damaged or disabled, fighting ships may well have remained
afloat until such time as they were broken up by waves, or
dashed to pieces against the shore. Moreover, if a badly holed
ship did find its way to the bottom, its sojourn on the sea-bed
would be brief, as it would be fully exposed, inside and out, to
the destructive attacks of the teredo and other marine borers.
The suggestion thus is that sunken warships of the Ancients are
not to be found because (1) undue exposure would soon bring
about their disintegration; or (2) their remains are completely
hidden by silt.

These are prospects which raise an important archaeological
issue: what crespuscular circumstances are necessary to assist
the preservation of a wooden ship during centuries of immersion,
and yet ensure that its presence remains detectable? The first
essential would appear to be that the covering of water must
not be too shallow—preferably not less than 100 feet in depth,
at which level a fabricated timber structure would be reasonably
safe, both from wave action and from notice by casual observers.
It is also desirable that the sinking should not take place in or
near a busy harbour, where the existence of a wreck would be
known and its presence might constitute a danger to other
shipping, a situation which would call for its removal. Rather is
it preferable that the scene of any disaster should be in the
neighbourhood of an uninhabited stretch of coast, and that the
event should take place in the absence of witnesses or survivors,
lest their testimony result in attempts at salvage. And once
underwater, it is necessary that a wreck should be shielded
from the various agencies which would otherwise bring about
its eventual destruction. As a means to this conservational end,
it would be advantageous if the vessel happened to be a fully
laden merchantman (as its cargo would afford internal protection), and if it came to rest on a layer of mud or sand, by which
(in part thanks to its weight) it would tend gradually to become
enveloped. Less satisfactory is the possibility that the ship might
settle on a surface of bare and unyielding rock or, at the other
extreme, on a bed of mud so soft and deep that it was engulfed
without leaving any trace.

In practice, it is usual to find (understandably enough, since
it is a prerequisite of the discovery) that a cargo ship has

become covered over only in part, and that, following the collapse of its exposed upper structure, it has assumed the appearance of a low-lying mound. Left undisturbed, such a monticulate burial will afford protection to its contents indefinitely, but may well reveal its identity by providing a glimpse of the topmost layer of its displaced cargo. This, then, is all that is likely to mark the grave of an Ancient Greek or Roman merchantman—a squat and seemingly insignificant tumulus, meaningful only to the eye of an experienced observer, unless it happens to be visibly capped by an array of unmistakably man-made objects.

Even what at first sight appears to be such an indication, however, does not necessarily betoken the presence of a sunken vessel. It may merely mark the (archaeologically valuable, since if undisturbed it will be stratified) site of a much used shelter from storms, a haven which served as a convenient place for the disposal of unwanted rubbish, in which event it should also provide a plentiful supply of discarded anchors. For the ships of antiquity, because of their lack of manœuvrability (aggravated by an inability to sail against the wind) needed to rely heavily upon some form of retaining device, especially if they happened to be caught offshore in bad weather, and it is known that the carrying of a score or more anchors was by no means unusual. From examples of these items already recovered, their lavish use (and frequent loss) would appear to date from at least the seventh century B.C., an early form consisting of a block of stone, shaped and pierced to take a rope, though by Roman times this had become a wooden shank weighted with as much as half a ton of lead.

V

Sinkings in the Mediterranean, of course, did not cease with the collapse of the western half of the Roman Empire in the fifth century A.D.—the power thus relinquished continued to be exercised, albeit in an increasingly Hellenistic guise, by the Byzantine rulers in the East, at sea as well as on land. Their naval forces came to be equipped with pamphylians and dromonds, fast biremes capable of carrying as many as 300 sailors and marines, and in an attempt to deny similar facilities to the enemy, the Emperor Justinian (527–565) decreed that an artisan who imparted his knowledge of shipbuilding to an unskilled barbarian was liable to suffer the death penalty. But despite this prohibition, the Arab adherents of Islam emerged as a formidable maritime nation, able and willing under the leadership of Mo'awiya, the first of the Omayyad Caliphs, to make a prolonged assault upon Constantinople. When this near impregnable capital fortress finally fell to the *Sarraceni*, however, it was to the armed forces of Sultan Mohamet II nearly eight centuries later, by which time (1453) the failure of the Crusades had left the Moslems in control of the greater part of the *Mare Internum*.

Subsequent events in the area belong to the period of modern history, though this is not to say that these more recent times are so fully documented that no additional information relating to them is either desired or needed. Surprising though it may seem, a great deal has yet to be learned about the precise mode of construction of sailing craft built 300, let alone 3,000 years ago, thanks to a paucity of detailed plans which, even if they were ever prepared and used, seldom appear to have been kept. In any case, the recent happenings of yesterday inevitably become the remote occurrences of tomorrow, and while it may be conceded that any expression of archaeological interest in the remains of the Italian warships sunk by British forces during the Battle of Cape Matapan in 1941 would be somewhat premature at the present moment, this is a situation which may be expected to change as time goes by. In the years ahead, indeed, it is possible that these and other twentieth century underwater relics (in company with certain extra-terrestrial items*) will

---

*It is an interesting speculation that, by the twenty-first century, archaeologists will be making an environmental distinction, not only between the activities they carry out on land and under the sea, but also in space. Since 4 October, 1957, when the Russians placed Sputnik I in orbit, thousands of other man-made objects have been hurled aloft, of which about half still remain there, pending their eventual destruction by incineration as they re-enter the earth's atmosphere, or plunge into the sun. Much of this encircling debris (and of that which is destined to be added to it in the years ahead) may be expected to continue to fulfil the role of minor members of the solar system for an appreciable period of time, and it would be surprising indeed if these artifacts failed to excite the curiosity and interest of our descendants, by whom they will doubtless be tracked down, captured, and brought back to earth for detailed examination and study. Archaeological excursions to the moon and the planets for the purpose of excavating wrecked or abandoned vehicles relating to the early Space Age may also be envisaged as a prospect of the future.

provide the only tangible evidence of the former existence of supposedly civilized nations whose self-inflicted obliteration by thermo-nuclear devices was otherwise complete.

Meanwhile, in so far as marine archaeology is concerned, the Mediterranean is unique, and it is no accident that it has become the acknowledged centre of underwater activity. Not only is its floor virtually the sole repository of the sunken shipping of the Ancients, but it is also the resting place of a representative selection of vessels belonging to medieval and modern times, thus providing an unbroken maritime sequence of some 5,000 years. Over this period, the freight of wrecked cargo carriers alone promises to furnish investigators with collections of cultural material, the like of which is not to be found anywhere on land—or beneath any other body of water.

However, there exist two other seas of possible archaeological interest which share some of the distinctive geographic characteristics of the Mediterranean, if not its unrivalled historical associations—the Caribbean and the Baltic. Of these, the Caribbean, situated, appropriately enough, at the opposite end of what used to be the Tethys Sea, comprises an embayed area whose mainland borders are the equatorial extremities of the two Americas, North and South. Today, these continents are, of course, joined by the Isthmus of Panama (though this was not always the case—up to a million or so years ago, the Isthmus was represented by a string of volcanic islands, round which the waters of the Atlantic and Pacific Oceans surged and mingled), while on the remaining side, the encirclement is completed by the West Indian archipelago, extending from the Yucatan peninsula (Mexico), by way of Cuba, Hispaniola, and the Lesser Antilles to the coast of Venezeula.

The region thus enclosed, though in places much deeper than the Mediterranean, nevertheless bears a remarkable resemblance to that sea in a number of ways. Its area is of the same order (in the vicinity of a million square miles), and tidal movement is negligible. Again, its floor consists of a series of depressions separated by submarine ridges, one of which forms the dividing line between an eastern and a smaller western part (the Cayman Sea). Nor do the similarities merely consist of physical features. In company with its Old World counterpart, the Caribbean can claim a melancholy list of ship sinkings, headed by the *Santa Maria* of Christopher Columbus, which was wrecked off Hispaniola soon after the discoverer first reached that island in 1492. With the subsequent arrival of the *conquistadores*, a wholesale plundering of the mainland ensued, and much of the booty (including the royal fifth) was shipped to the homeland of the invaders, in this instance in fleets of Spanish galleons whose course took them across the Caribbean, as a preliminary to the start of their transatlantic journey.

It was while the treasure laden vessels were in Caribbean waters that the threat of interception and attack was most acute, and it was the French who were the first to take advantage of the situation. In this profitable enterprise they were soon joined by the British and the Dutch, and later by those gentlemen of fortune of many nationalities, the buccaneers. These piratical activities undoubtedly resulted in the capture and sinking of many a rich prize—though not, it seems prudent to assume, before their holds had been emptied of everything of value they contained.

Spanish reaction to this unwelcome turn of events was to form fleets of merchantmen and give them the protection of warships, and once the worth of the system had been demonstrated, sailing in convoy was made compulsory (*cedula* of July, 1561). But in seeking to ensure the safety of their vessels from enemy attack by herding them together, the Spanish authorities collectively exposed them to another and no less dangerous hazard, against which they could provide no defence. This took the form of highly destructive wind storms, which sprang up without warning and blew at speeds of up to 150 miles an hour. As was soon learned, to place a convoy of ships in the path of one of these hurricanes was to invite a major disaster, such as that which resulted in the loss of 15 plate ships and their escorts in the great storm of 1542. . . .

Although the wreck of a sixteenth century Spanish galleon is likely to command less academic interest than the remains of an Ancient Greek or Roman cargo carrier, it is nevertheless to be expected that the Caribbean, hitherto the domain of the treasure seeker, will eventually claim its due share of attention from the underwater archaeologist—and perhaps none too soon. Already the scramble to find Spanish doubloons and

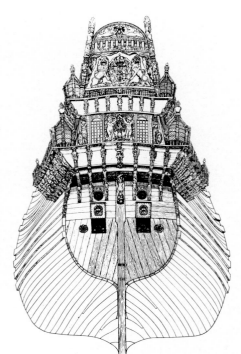

14. (*right*) reconstruction of the *Vasa*'s stern, drawn by the artist Gunnar Olofsson, of Stockholm. 15. (*below*) The *Vasa* of 1628, with a displacement of some 1,300 tons—a drawing by Nils Stödberg. (Photos: *Maritime Museum and the warship* Vasa)

16. Tollund Man. During the past two centuries, the property of the tannic acid content of peat bogs to prevent organic decay has been demonstrated by the finding of scores of bodies in the Jutland and Schleswig-Holstein areas. In 1950, the particularly well preserved remains of an Early Iron Age man, who died some 2,000 years ago, were recovered from Tollund Mose, a bog set among the hills in the vicinity of Aarhus, Jutland. That the Tollund Man had been hanged—possibly the victim of a ritual sacrifice—was evident from part of a braided leather rope which still encircled his neck. (Photo: *Nationalmuseet, Copenhagen*)

pieces of eight has been going on for three centuries or more, to the detriment of not a few accessible sites. As early as 1687, a sunken galleon located by members of the William Phipps expedition yielded a fortune in gold ingots, bars of silver, and jewels, and this despite the fact that worsening weather, sickness amongst the crew, and the threat of pirates brought the work of recovery to a premature stop, so that half the precious cargo had to be left behind. However, when, in 1933, the late A. H. Verrill[140] and some companions sought to retrieve the abandoned treasure, an unexpected problem was encountered: during its long immersion, the wreck had become encased in a concrete-like shell of limestone, upwards of two feet in thickness! Thus the circumstance that the waters of the region are sufficiently warm to sustain the growth of coral promises greatly to add to the problems of location and recovery which will face would-be investigators of the future.

As for the Baltic, this intra-continental sea was also the scene of intensive maritime activity during the sixteenth and seventeenth centuries, and it, too, is known to contain wrecks of historical interest. It is also possessed of an important advantage, not shared by either the Mediterranean or the Caribbean, which stems from the fact that it drains an area of the land enclosing it which is four times greater in extent than itself. As a result, its constantly replenished contents are maintained at a slightly higher level than that of the North Sea into which it empties, as a consequence of which it constitutes the largest body of brackish water in the world.

The far-reaching archaeological implications of this first appear to have occurred to Anders Franzen, a Swedish exponent. It was he, at all events, who perceived that because the salinity of the Baltic was below the crucial 0·04 per cent necessary for the existence of the teredo shipworm, the absence of this highly destructive mollusc would greatly increase the life expectancy of any wooden ship immersed in its waters. And the outcome of this realization, as Franzen[58] has himself described, was that it led him to make an inventory of a dozen or so vessels which the official records named as having foundered in the area, among them the *Lybska Svan*, the *Mars*, the *Lybska Orn*, the *Riksvasa*, the *Riksnyckeln*, the *Vasa*. . . .

VI

The last-named was one of a number of warships built at the instigation of Gustavus II Adolphus of Sweden (1611–1632), whose royal purpose was the frustration of Hapsburg ambitions to dominate the Baltic. The vessel was launched in 1627 and fitted out in the following year, her armament consisting of 64 bronze cannon, collectively weighing some 80 tons. The maiden voyage, however, was of brief duration. While still within Stockholm harbour, and after sailing no more than a few hundred yards, the ship heeled over in a sudden squall, and sank in 100 feet of water, leaving only the tops of several masts showing.

Unsuccessful attempts to raise the vessel followed, in the course of which, thanks to the combined efforts of Hans Albrekt von Treileban (himself a Swede) and Andreas Peckall (a German), the *Vasa* was at any rate relieved of the weight of many cannon. The not inconsiderable feat of extracting and lifting these heavy guns was accomplished by leather-clad operators who made the descent in a diving bell, of a size which sufficed for a working time of about 15 minutes, a period afterwards increased by sending down additional supplies of air in a cask (Halley system). But any hope of salvaging the ship itself was eventually abandoned, and the vessel gradually sank deeper and deeper into the mud until not only its whereabouts, but even its presence in the harbour, came to be forgotten.

In 1920, the fouling of an anchor led to the discovery of (what proved to be) the remains of the warship *Riksnyckeln*, which had also been lost in the year 1628. And it was during the subsequent examination of the Swedish State archives, which led to the identifying of this particular wreck, that the existence of the *Vasa* came to light, together with details of the sinking, the circumstances of which decided Anders Franzen to try to locate this new and undamaged vessel.

The information at his disposal inclined him to the view that the task should not prove to be too difficult, particularly as the disaster had occurred within the confines of Stockholm harbour. But the continued lack of success which attended his efforts suggested otherwise. Summer after summer, he found himself engaged in a seemingly fruitless quest, as he traversed back and forth in a motor boat, trailing grapnels and wire sweeps. Moreover, so numerous were the unseen objects which were encountered in the muddy water that an individual examination of each obstruction by divers was out of the question, a problem which Franzen answered by devising an underwater core sampler, in its essentials a tube with a cutting edge.

It was during the winter of 1955–6 that his literary researches produced a letter in which the island of Beckholmen was named as being close to the scene of the disaster. Armed with this information, and the knowledge that the sinking had taken place in 100 feet of water, Franzen (after allowing for subsequent sedimentation) drew a contour line on a map of the area, and began making soundings with his sampler. And on a day in August, 1956, the instrument brought up the first of a series of pieces of darkened oak which, on investigation, proved to have come from the missing ship.

A Committee was formed to consider the possibilities of salvage, to which end Navy divers armed with powerful water jets drove six tunnels under the vessel. Steel cables attached to pontoons were next passed under the wreck; the floats were filled with water and the cables tightened; the water was pumped out of the floats and the *Vasa* lifted clear of the sea-bed, to be towed towards a shallower region until grounding occurred. The operation was then repeated many times until, after the hulk had been caulked and pumped dry, it finally broke surface.

More than a thousand ornamental and other timber details which had detached themselves from the *Vasa*'s exterior were also recovered, and much experimentation was done to determine how the wood of these items, and that of the ship itself could best be preserved. In the course of drying, waterlogged timber tends to crack and warp, and a way of preventing this is to provide a substitute for the fluid that is lost by evaporation, thus reinforcing the cellular structure of the wood and so inhibiting undue shrinkage. The substances which gave the best results were the water-soluble polyethylene glycols, a series of high molecular alcohols ranging from viscous liquids to wax-like solids.

Nor was timber the only material which required treatment.

Apart from a number of other organic substances (bone, leather, paper, horn, ivory, tortoise-shell), some of which were also likely to benefit from the glycol process, many metal items were found, made of silver, bronze, pewter, and iron. The non-ferrous variety, as was to be expected, were the least affected by immersion, whereas objects of iron tended to disintegrate when exposed to the air. In an elaborate process designed to arrest such deterioration, the object is subjected to a protracted soaking in a solution of sodium hydroxide, after which it is brought into contact with a reducing (oxygen absorbing) agent, e.g., metallic zinc. This is followed by extensive washing in distilled water, heating in an oven, and treatment with phosphoric acid. It should be added that the baking of iron cannonballs can be a hazardous undertaking: it is by no means unknown for some of these supposedly solid missiles to turn out to be hollow spheres filled with gunpowder!

With the raising of the *Vasa*, the year 1961 saw the culmination of what was undoubtedly an outstanding achievement in the realm of undersea rescue. Yet surprisingly, having regard for all the circumstances of an undertaking which concerned a known wreck in a (more or less) known position, the exercise clearly demonstrated that the difficulties involved in the recovery of such a find were more than likely to be matched by the problem of locating it. However, enclosed seas are by no means the only bodies of water which are of interest to the archaeologist. Submerged sites are also to be found inland, in situations which often offer the double advantage of limited extent and shallowness of depth. In circumstances such as these, the inhabitants of the region may well be aware of the presence of drowned structures and the like, if not by personal observation, then at any rate by repute. So it is not altogether a matter for astonishment that, in addition to the annals of marine salvage, the origins of underwater archaeology are also to be found in a series of lacrustine events, inspired by local knowledge and tradition.

Chapter Four

Tentative Beginnings

I

According to the researches of Guido Ucelli,[139] early in the fifteenth century a certain Cardinal Colonna gathered together such information as was then available about a pair of Ancient Roman galleys known to be resting on the bottom of Lake Nemi, a water-filled volcanic crater located in the Alban Hills, some 14 miles south-east of Rome. In 1446, the Cardinal's interest led to the making of the first recorded attempt to raise the vessels, when an architect named Leon Battista Alberti engaged swimmers from Genoa to assist him in the undertaking. But although a raft of barrels was constructed, from which ropes were attached to hooks in one of the wrecks, all efforts to pull the boat closer inshore failed.

The next investigation of the site would appear to be that carried out by Guglielmo de Lorena during the early 1530s, in association with Francesco de Marchi, an author who later published an account of the enterprise. Although nothing came of it, the undertaking was notable in that Lorena made his descent wearing a wooden hood, large enough to envelop his head and the upper part of his body. This primitive diving helmet was fitted with a window, and was designed to rest on the shoulders, additional support being provided by slings. According to de Marchi his colleague was able to remain under water for an hour or more at a time, thanks to a periodic replenishment of the air supply. Precisely how this was accomplished, however, the writer does not say, as he had been enjoined by his companion to keep silent on this point.

After this attempt, nearly three centuries were to elapse before Annesio Fusconi arrived on the scene, equipped with a more sophisticated piece of apparatus. This took the form of an outsize diving bell, whose seating capacity of eight enabled his underwater activities to be watched by a small but distinguished audience of noblemen and diplomats. As before, however, efforts to move one of the silted-up ships merely resulted in the tearing away of portions of its hull, a process which was continued in 1895 by Eliseo Borghi, a dealer in antiquities. He arrived at Lake Nemi from Rome with a diving companion, with whose aid he was able to retrieve sundry objects, ranging from a large piece of mosaic decking and a length of lead water-pipe to a quantity of tiles and a number of bronze animal heads, holding rings in their teeth. Some of these items were sold to the Government at prices which the purchasers considered so outrageously high that any further work at the site was officially banned. At this juncture, an interesting suggestion was made to the Authorities: Why not drain the lake?

In the event, this imaginative proposal had to await the coming to power of Benito Mussolini, who put the plan into operation five years after making himself master of Italy in 1923. The project was helped very considerably by the existence of a mile-long overflow tunnel, dating from Roman times, and pumping, once begun, was continued for the next four years, at the end of which period the water level had been lowered by more than 70 feet, sufficient fully to expose the two vessels. The delicate task of freeing their remains from the mud and debris in which they were embedded was accomplished by means of non-metallic implements. This ensured that the minimum amount of damage was done to the fragile timbers, which were shored up as the work progressed. As an added precaution, the woodwork was maintained in a damp condition, so as to avoid shrinkage and warping.

Although the remains of the two craft fell somewhat short of Mussolini's hopeful expectation that they would be revealed as 'immense and superb vessels, with rooms and gardens and fountains, ornamented with marbles and precious metals and rare woods, all shining with gold and purple', he was at any rate not disappointed in his estimation of their size. The length of one boat was 234 feet and that of its companion 239 feet, with beams which measured 66 and 78 feet respectively. It was evident, moreover, that they had been built in a most sumptuous fashion, replete with private cabins and bathing facilities, their upper decks supported by fluted marble columns, and it has been surmised that their function had been to serve as imperial pleasure barges. The only tangible clue to the name of the royal owner was provided by a piece of lead pipe, which bore the name *Caligula* (A.D. 37–41). This suggests that the vessels were in use either during the short reign of this monarch, or that of his successor Claudius (A.D. 41–54), though for reasons which are not explained, R. H. Davis[41] and others[34] ascribe ownership to the Emperor Trajan (A.D. 98 – 117).

The two ships, their hulls remarkably well preserved by the mud in which they had lain down through the centuries, were carefully removed and housed in a museum erected on the shore of the lake, there to be examined at leisure and in more detail. In the course of this investigation, some ingenious contrivances were found, among them a bilge cleaning device, consisting of buckets on an endless chain, and an anchor fitted with a movable stock, designed to increase its holding power (an idea considered sufficiently novel and promising for it to be patented by the British Admiralty some 2000 years later!). Another surprise was the discovery that the hulls of the two vessels, in the manner of sea-going craft of the period, had been sheathed with lead below the waterline, as a protection against non-existant teredoes.

Presumably the ships were sunk—and thus unintentionally preserved for posterity—during the period of the Empire's decline which culminated in the sacking of Rome. There is thus considerable irony in the fact that their salvaged remains were not destined to survive the arrival in Italy of the modern descendants of the Germanic *barbari* of the fifth century A.D. At all events, on 31 May 1944, unappreciative members of the

retreating Wehrmacht wantonly set alight to the remains of
the two boats, and reduced them to ashes.

II

The circumstance that lakes are to be found throughout most
of the habitable regions of the earth's surface, and that since
time immemorial they have tended to attract settlers to their
shores, makes their waters a promising source of archaeological
material. As to this, an interesting pointer was long ago
provided by Herodotus,[71] in his account of those inhabitants
of Thessaly who lived in the vicinity of Lake Prasias in the
fifth century B.C.:

> Their manner of living is the following. Platforms supported
> upon tall pines stand in the middle of the lake, which are
> approached from the land by a single narrow bridge. At first the
> piles which bear up the platforms were fixed in their places by the
> whole body of the citizens, but since that time the custom which
> has prevailed about fixing them is this: they are brought from a
> hill called Orbelus, and every man drives in three for each wife
> that he marries. Now the men have all many wives apiece; and
> this is the way in which they live. Each has his own hut, wherein
> he dwells, upon one of the platforms, and each has also a trap
> door giving access to the lake beneath; and their wont is to tie
> their baby children by the foot with a string, to save them from
> rolling into the water.

While there is now some doubt as to the precise location and
identity of both Lake Prasias and Mount Orbelus, the worth of
these observations was seemingly established by a series of
discoveries which took place in Alpine Europe from the 1830s
onwards. After two bronze swords and the remains of a canoe
had been dredged up at Concise, on Lake Neuchâtel, local
fishermen reported encountering a forest of underwater
obstructions in a number of other lakes, though no explanation
of the phenomenon was immediately forthcoming. For this,
they had to await the winter of 1853–54, in which year the
seasonal diminution in the amount of melt-water reaching the
valleys from the surrounding snow-clad mountains was much
greater than usual. As a result, lake levels fell to an unprecedented extent, and in places local residents sought to take

advantage of the situation by building retaining walls on the newly exposed territory, that they might thereby extend their vineyards. And it was while in the course of so doing that workmen at Ober-Meilen, on the east shore of Lake Zürich, came upon the heads of wooden piles projecting out of the mud, around which were scattered the remains of pottery, together with stone axes and other implements. The find was considered sufficiently important to merit bringing it to the attention of Dr. Ferdinand Keller, of Zürich, who, after making extensive investigations, reached the considered conclusion, announced in a series of memoirs presented to the Anthropological Society of his home town, that it had been the custom among the early inhabitants of the region to erect their dwellings, not on firm ground at the lakeside, but on elevated platforms located above the surface of the water.

The widespread nature of this supposed practice was revealed some 30 years later. In 1868, there had been begun an ambitious hydrological project (the *Correction des Eaux du Jura*) intended to improve the natural drainage system which existed between the three inter-connected lakes of Bienne, Morat, and Neu-châtel. The eventual outcome was that the waters of the last-named were lowered by about nine feet, to disclose the remnants of many more pile dwellings—in all, more than 100 individual settlements were exposed, dating from early Neolithic times (4000 B.C.) to the Late Bronze Age (700 B.C.). Nor were such habitations confined to Switzerland, for similar sites were discovered along the borders of lakes in west France, north Italy, and south-west Germany.

Excavations carried out by R. R. Schmidt and H. Reinerth on the shore of the Federsee, in Wurttemberg, however, established that in this instance, the piles had unmistakably served as stakes which held in place insulating layers of timber and bark, laid as a floor covering on ground which was marshy at a time when the level of the lake was lower than it is today. And this interpretation, it is now generally agreed, is applicable to most, if not all, similar groups of Alpine dwellings. But the value of the sites, irrespective of their exact location, was that they had been situated, if not actually over stagnant water, then at any rate on ground sufficiently humid for it to have ensured the preservation of wood and other perishable substances by

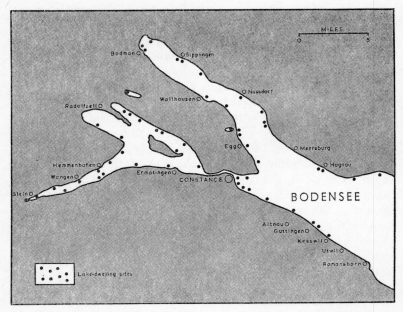

21. Sites of pile dwellings in the Bodensee, Untersee, and Ueberlinger See areas of Lake Constance (after R. Munro).

the exclusion of air, thereby inhibiting destructive oxidation. Hitherto, cultural objects relating to prehistoric man in Europe had been restricted to imperishable items such as stone and metal tools, but now artifacts of a normally much less durable nature had unexpectedly come to light, among them wooden implements (such as ladles) and weapons (including self-bows), together with fragments of woven baskets, and even pieces of linen. A fact of outstanding archaeological importance thus emerged: in certain favourable circumstances, a moist or underwater site could be expected to provide examples of organic materials which, on land, would ordinarily have been found to have rotted away.

III

Although the majority of lakes are composed of fresh water some (such as the Dead so-called Sea) are excessively salt while others (among them the Caspian and Aral erstwhile Seas) actually were once a part of the ocean. Classification, however, is not based on the degree of salinity of their contents, but on a genetical basis, it being recognized that the mode of formation of an inland body of water may be distinguished as glacial, coastal, volcanic, alluvial, tectonic, relict, barrier, or karstic—this last description a reference to the now barren Karst district of western Yugoslavia where, thanks to subterranean drainage, underground solution cavities form, suffer roof collapse, and then collect water.

Closely akin to karstic lake formations are the natural wells which abound in the surface of the porous limestone of the Yucatan peninsula, in Mexico. Not a few of these features have diameters of 200 feet or more, and they are often possessed of precipitous sides which descend to considerable depths. In days gone by, in a region virtually devoid of surface rivers and streams, these *cenotes* provided the resident Maya population with their only source of drinking water. However, not every pit served this purpose, as some were set apart as the abode of the gods, and so became receptacles for sacrificial offerings, as the Spanish invaders learned, once they had succeeded in pacifying the inhabitants after a decade of bloody strife from 1527 onwards.

At once the most revered and the most renowned of these sacred water holes was that which existed within the bounds of the capital city of Chitzen Itza (pronounced Cheechan Eet-za, and meaning 'The rim of the well of the Itza'), about which Diego de Landa, the second Bishop of Yucatan, reported in 1566:

> Into this Well they have had and still have the custom of throwing men alive as a sacrifice to their gods in time of drought, and they believe that they would not die, though they never saw them again. They also threw in many other things like precious stones and things they prized, and if this country had possessed gold it would have been this Well that would have the greater part of it, so great is the devotion that the Indians show for it.

This account, contained in de Landa's *Relación de las Cosas de Yucatan*, was filed away and forgotten until its discovery in the Royal Library of Madrid in 1864, when its contents aroused much interest and speculation. A tentative attempt to dredge the well was made by a French investigator as early as 1882, though with unsuitable equipment and small success. Meanwhile, a copy of the long lost report had come into the possession of Edward Herbert Thompson,[135] an American who, on reading the story of the well of sacrifice, became obsessed with the idea of probing its mysteries, an ambition which was furthered by his obtaining a U.S. Consular post in Yucatan. Thereafter, as Arthur Evans had done in Crete before him, he made an outright purchase of the site of his choice (for which, including the ruins of the city, he paid the equivalent of seventy-five U.S. dollars!), that the recovery work he planned might be carried out untroubled by disputes over ownership—a wise precaution, as will later be seen. His preparations also entailed a visit to Boston, where he took lessons in deep-sea diving, and set about acquiring a bucket dredge and winch, complete with tackles, steel cables, and a derrick fitted with a 30-foot swinging boom. His next move was to approach influential members of the American Antiquarian Society, as a result of which, not only did he enlist the support of Charles P. Bowditch, but he gained the sponsorship of Harvard University's Peabody Museum.

Back in the jungle, the new owner of the extensive Chitchen plantation surveyed the remains of the ancient city he had acquired. From the steps of the Temple of Kukil Can, a processional way led to the edge of the sacrificial well, itself a steeply-sided, oval-shaped opening measuring 200 feet across at its widest part, and some 140 feet deep. In common with other *cenotes* of the region, the point at which the shaft intercepted the prevailing water table was indicated by the presence of a pool, the level of which was maintained about half way up the shaft from an underground stream. At this time (1904), the well contained some 35 feet of water atop another 35 feet or so of mud, and in order to facilitate the removal of this sludge, Thompson so arranged his equipment that the bucket could be lowered into any selected area of the water by controlling its lateral movement with the aid of guide ropes. He then enacted a macabre simulation of the priestly rites of propitiation by casting heavy objects into the pool in an attempt to establish where the remains of any victims would be most likely to be found. Dredging then began.

As each bucket-load of sediment was raised from the depths, it was deposited near the edge of the well and examined for objects of interest. But for days, all that was recovered was a mixture of slime and rocks. Then oddments of broken pottery began to appear, promising pieces of evidence which were eventually accompanied by two globular yellow masses of incense. At this, Thompson resigned his consular appointment, that he might be free to give his undivided attention to his self-imposed task. Nor did this expression of confidence prove to be unjustified. From then on, a seemingly endless array of objects began to arrive at the surface, among which were temple vases and incense burners, lance points and arrow heads, hammer stones and copper chisels, beads and pendants. In addition, many offerings of jade, and of (mostly low grade) gold were found, the metal items appearing in the guise of basins, rings, and statuettes, not to mention a throwing stick and a face mask. Some of the gold was in sheet form, impressed with scenes of battle and sacrificial rites, in one of which a priest was depicted in the act of cutting out the living heart of a victim. And seemingly in confirmation of the tradition that the well had played a part in such ceremonies, also recovered from its depths were parts of human skeletons, both male and female —these last, it was romantically to be supposed, the remains of young maidens selected at times of acute drought to satisfy the carnal appetite of one Chac, a long-nosed rain god.

When at last the bucket began to come up empty, Thompson donned his diving dress and descended into the muddy waters, now more than 60 feet deep. He was assisted in this more difficult part of the undertaking by two Greek sponge divers, but as total darkness was encountered after the first few feet, in which blackness flashlights proved useless, all the three men had to rely upon was their sense of touch, and the operation yielded little that was new in the way of finds. But although at this point his underwater activities came to an end, Thompson afterwards expressed the conviction that the sacred well had by no means given up the last of its secrets:

With all the precious objects I have taken by force from the Rain God, I am very sure that I have wrested from him not a tenth of his jealously held treasure. There are many, many more golden ornaments hid away in the recesses of the uneven floor of the pit, and many, many things even more priceless than gold to the antiquarian.

The results of Thompson's work at Chitchen Itza have been variously assessed. As an archaeological exercise his efforts undoubtedly left much to be desired, though with the primitive means at his disposal, this could hardly have been otherwise. But the orderless manner of their recovery apart, the materials he salvaged certainly proved to be of some scientific interest and value. Apart from losses occasioned by theft at the site (where, it transpired, a rival investigator had been bribing workers to steal from their employer!), most of the items went to the Peabody Museum, there to form the nucleus of what Alfred M. Tozzer, a resident authority, described as a unique collection of Maya artifacts. As for the value of the display, an aggrieved Mexican Government, after becoming aware of the extent of its loss following the publication, in 1923, of an interview with Thompson in *The New York Times Magazine*, placed this at two million dollars and began a legal battle aimed at the recovery of this sum, failing the prompt return of its national treasures. The ensuing litigation finally reached the highest court in the land, and the outcome was a reluctant admission that at the time of the alleged offence, the defendant had infringed no law then existing in respect of the exportation of valuable objects found on property of which he was the rightful owner. An offer made by the Museum in the 1930s, voluntarily to hand over half of the finds, was not accepted, since when (1959), as a good will gesture to mark the occasion of the 58th Congress of American Anthropologists, 94 items of gold were returned to the land of their origin. As to this, apart from the unavailable calcium content of its limestone, Yucatan is a non-metalliferous region, from which it is evident that any gold and copper artifacts retrieved from the well must have been offerings brought into the district by pilgrims. And in many instances, typological considerations indicated the probable place of manufacture, while chemical analysis revealed from which areas the metals had been mined, so establishing the existence of a widespread trade in raw materials and finished products.

For the rest, much of the archaeological value of the finds, as

in the case of those associated with the Swiss lakeside settlements, lay in the fact that not a few of them consisted of
organic materials, not normally encountered during land
excavations, which owed their preservation to their immersion
—wooden spears, weaving tools, ceremonial rattles, head-
dresses, and, by no means least, fragments of pre-Columbian
fabrics which, as the only examples of their kind known,
provided otherwise unobtainable information about cloth
manufacture among the Itzas.

IV

An interest in marine, as opposed to the more restricted inland
(and mainly freshwater) archaeological sites, may be traced to
the activities of Guiseppe de Fazio, an Italian engineer. A
century or so ago, with the help of resident sponge divers, he
investigated the submerged remains of the ancient Mediterranean ports of Misenum and Pozzuoli, and as a result of his
findings, reached the conclusion that the region must have
undergone considerable changes in level since Roman times.
Thus at Pozzuoli, while examining the base of massive piers
which formed part of a breakwater, he came upon mooring
rings 6 feet below the surface, indicative of a subsidence of 10
feet or so. Nor was this all, for evidence of an equally extensive
movement in the opposite direction was provided by the outer-
most pier, which showed signs of biological activity well above
the then existing waterline.

These findings (attributable to localized land movements
rather than to alterations in sea level) were subsequently
confirmed by R. T. Gunther, a Fellow of Oxford, who also
made an extensive survey of the same area during the years
1901–3. Aided, like his predecessor, by the knowledge of the
fishermen of the district, and with the added assistance of a
glass-bottomed boat, he was able to map the ruins of innumerable drowned villas, and to deduce, not only that in Roman
times the land level was many feet higher than it is today, but
that, after attaining a lower level, it had risen again to its
present height—a remarkable sequence of events seemingly
confirmed by erosion marks on the walls of the famous Blue
Grotto on the nearby Isle of Capri.

The attention of investigators next turned to the Afro-Asian shore of the Mediterranean where, in 1910, Gaston Jondet stumbled upon the remains of an ancient harbour in the Delta region of Egypt. It has been suggested that even 2,000 years ago, the builders of this immense undertaking had already been forgotten and were unknown, and that by the time Alexander the Great reached the vicinity in 332 B.C., intent upon establishing a new port to rival that of Tyre which he had that year had occasion to destroy, the walls of the age-old Egyptian anchorage had already sunk beneath the waves. On the other hand, it is possible that Homer[76] (c. 800 B.C.?) knew of its existence:

> There is an island called Pharos in the rolling seas off the mouth of the Nile, a day's sail out for a well-found vessel with a roaring wind astern. In this island is a sheltered cove where sailors come to draw their water from a well and can launch their boats on an even keel into the deep sea.

The channel which then separated Pharos from the mainland has since become silted up, and the onetime island is now the promontory of Ras-el-Tin. But in days gone by, when Pharos was surrounded by water, a harbour was formed by linking the island with (what is now known as) the rock of Abu Bakar. To this end, the builders erected a double line of breakwaters, in this manner forming an inner and an outer haven which together enclosed an area of more than 300 acres. In tracing the course of these structures, Jondet was suitably impressed by their dimensions—each had a length of 8,500 feet, a width of 200 feet, and was 30 feet high. No mortar or cement had been used in the construction, which consisted of thick facing walls of massive limestone blocks, evidently quarried from the nearby villages of Mex and Dekhela. The tops of the structures, moreover, were capped by outsize flagstones, some of which were laid in a pattern reminiscent of the island of Crete. For this reason, the discoverer, in his report (*Les Ports Submergés de l'Ancienne Île de Pharos*, Le Caire, 1916) ascribed authorship to the Minoans. It is inconceivable, however, that so extensive an undertaking, with its multitude of associated wharfs and quays, could have been completed without the consent and co-operation of the reigning Pharaoh, just as in later years the founding of the Greek trading post of Naucratis on the banks of

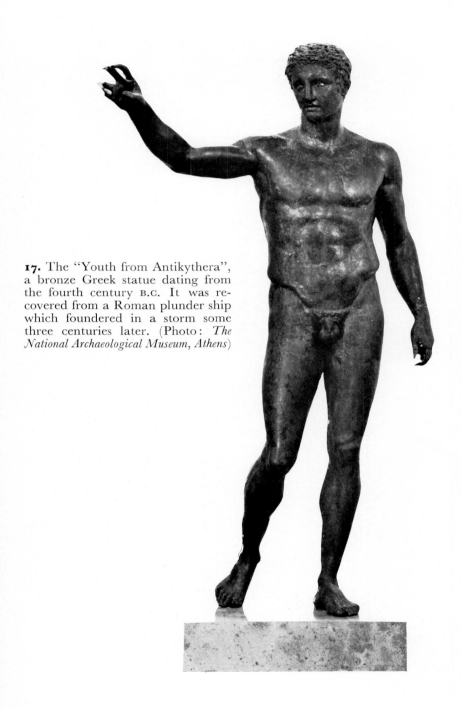

17. The "Youth from Antikythera",
a bronze Greek statue dating from
the fourth century B.C. It was recovered from a Roman plunder ship
which foundered in a storm some
three centuries later. (Photo: *The
National Archaeological Museum, Athens*)

18, 19. Bronze statues recovered from the wreck at Mahdia—Eros and a satyr. (Photos: *The National Museum, Le Bardo, Tunis*)

the Nile in 640 B.C. was encouraged by Psammethichus I. But the name of the Egyptian ruler who countenanced the construction of the Great Harbour at Pharos is lost, as the event seemingly went unrecorded. On the admittedly slender evidence of some statues discovered at the adjacent settlement of Rhakotis, E. M. Forster[56] has suggested that Ramses II (1292–25 B.C.) may have been the monarch concerned, though it hardly seems likely that this boastful individual would have played a part in so important an undertaking without informing the world of the fact, if his interminable accounts of his supposed victory over the Hittites at the Battle of Kadesh are anything to go by.* Moreover, if Jondet is correct in his assumption of Minoan associations, an Egyptian king of earlier date would seem to be indicated—as far back as the start of the twelfth dynasty (2000 B.C.) in the view of one authority. But at the other extreme, Joan du Plat Taylor[134] is of the opinion that these supposedly pre-Alexandrine remains may well be of Roman date.

Meanwhile, the discovery and investigation of the harbour works at Pharos were followed by the making of a detailed examination of similar facilities associated with the neighbouring Phoenician seaport of Tyrus (Tyre), whose origins are likewise lost in antiquity, but concerning whose subsequent history at least something is known. According to the historian Josephus, the acknowledged 'Mother of Tyre' was the nearby town of Sidon, itself allegedly founded by a grandson of Noah. Justin, in echoing the tradition that Tyre was established by Sidonians driven out of their homes by the King of Ascalon, gives the date of this occurrence as one year before the fall of Troy (c. 1200 B.C.). It has since transpired, however, that both places were in existence prior to 1400 B.C., in as much as they

---

*At the Battle of Kadesh-on-the-Orontes, Egyptian fought Hittite for possession of Syria, and during the encounter, Ramses and some of his charioteers found themselves outmanoeuvred and surrounded, from which predicament they managed to extricate themselves by boldly charging through the ranks of the encircling enemy.

The eventual outcome was the signing of a peace treaty which left the Hittites in control of most of the disputed territory, though this did not prevent the result of the struggle from being presented to the Egyptian people as a great pharaonic victory. In successive official accounts, the story is progressively elaborated, gaining so extensively in the telling that in the end we find Ramses asserting, not only that the Hittites were wiped out to the last man, but that he personally disposed of each and every one of them!

8

find mention in the Tell el Amarna Letters. At this time, as a dependency of Egypt, Tyre was already possessed of a dockyard area based on a pair of offshore islands, and in later years the port flourished to such an extent that it emerged as the leading city of Phoenicia and the seat of its central government. Subsequently, mainland Tyre became known as Palaetryrus ('Old Tyre') when the two islands, after being connected by a mole, were occupied and fortified, a strategic move traditionally associated with King Hiram a contemporary of Solomon of Israel (*c.* 950 B.C.).

Thereafter, the inhabitants were able to defy or obtain favourable surrender terms from a succession of would-be conquerors, among them the Babylonian ruler Nebuchadnezzar II, whom they obliged to lay siege to their citadel for 13 years. But its reputation for impregnability was shattered within months of the arrival of Alexander the Great in 333 B.C. On its defiant occupants refusing his demand for submission, he organized a sea blockade, and after demolishing the town of Old Tyre, used the rubble to build a causeway to the island stronghold, so making possible its assault and capture. Some 8,000 of the defenders perished or were massacred during the attack, after which 2,000 more were summarily executed, and 30,000 others sold into slavery.

Although the captured city suffered no less grievously than its luckless inhabitants, it was afterwards rebuilt, to enjoy a measure of prosperity under the Seleucids and the Romans, though not to regain its former eminence, if only because it no longer possessed the immunity from attack it had for so long enjoyed—the causeway that had led to its downfall gradually accumulated sand, and so became a permanent feature. In A.D. 638, the place was occupied by Arab forces, and nearly five centuries passed before these intruders were ousted by the Crusaders, who stayed until the year 1291. The followers of Mohammed then took possession once more, and set about its methodical destruction. Today, under the Arabic name of Sur ('rock'), Tyre survives as a Lebanese town of no particular significance, and with few remaining signs of its former importance and renown.

A French archaeological expedition visited the neighbourhood in 1921, but it was left to Antione Poidebard, in the mid

1930s, to make a detailed investigation of the remnants of its harbour system. Prior to this, from 1925 onwards, Poidebard had interested himself in tracing the paths of caravan routes leading to the ruins of Roman frontier forts in the Syrian desert, in which task he was assisted by observations made from the air. This enterprise eventually brought him to the vicinity of Tyre, where aerial photography was also employed, with spectacular results.

When the survey of the ancient port began, the precise location of its docks and anchorages was not known, though Strabo[128] had provided the information that at the start of the first century A.D. two harbours were in use—one, known as the Egyptian port, which was open, and another which was closed, i.e., fortified. It seemed reasonable to suppose from the name bestowed upon it that the location of the Egyptian harbour was on the south side of the island, though as to its whereabouts, modern opinion tended to agree with Joseph Renan when he expressed the view (*Mission de Phenicie*, Paris, 1864) that it now lay beneath an adjacent wilderness of sand. Henry Maundrell,[150] however, an earlier and more perceptive observer who visited Tyre in 1697, after referring to the existence of an isthmus connecting the island to the shore as being

> covered all over with sand which the sea casts upon it as the tokens of its natural right to a passage there, from which it was, by Alexander the Great, injuriously excluded

goes on to describe how the onetime island fortress

> discovers still the foundations of a wall, which anciently encompassed it round at the utmost margin of the land. It makes, with the isthmus, two large bays, one on its north side and the other on its south. These bays are in part defended from the ocean, each by a long ridge, resembling a mole, stretching directly out, on both sides, from the head of the island, but these ridges, whether they were walls or rocks, whether the work of art or nature, I was too far distant to discern.

In fact, the ridges referred to were the work of nature embellished by the hand of man, as Poidebard discovered when he set about investigating the shadowy outlines which showed on his aerial photographs. He was fortunate in having the support of both the French and Lebanese authorities, who provided naval craft and helmeted Service divers to augment the underwater efforts of a number of sponge gatherers, recruited locally. With the aid of these considerable resources, a detailed survey of the entire port system was undertaken, and this disclosed that a line of submerged reefs, well over a mile long and running north and south at a tangent to the tip of the peninsula, had been artificially joined and heightened to form a massive breakwater which afforded protection to an extensive anchorage. In the course of centuries, much of this human handiwork had been swept away by the combined action of waves and swell, but on the inner face at the southern (Egyptian) end of the reef, foundation walls were discovered consisting of massive stone blocks (seemingly an importation), skilfully oriented so as to deflect silt-laden currents. An associated inner refuge had consisted of two enclosed basins, replete with quays. As for the closed (so-called Sidonian) harbour to the north of the island, this had incorporated a trio of docks served on the seaward side by an entrance sufficiently narrow (some 18 yards wide) for the admittance of unwelcome visitors to be denied by chain or other means.

With the publication of the results of his work (*Un grand port disparu: Tyr*, Paris, 1939), Poidebard not merely placed his findings on record, but he provided incontrovertible evidence of the feasibility of tracing (by means of aerial observation) and surveying (with the indispensable assistance of divers) an assemblage of drowned remains, and of undertaking their partial excavation, measurement, and photographic recording *in situ*.

V

Meanwhile, a dramatic sequence of events of archaeological import had been taking place in other and deeper parts of the Mediterranean. The first such happening, as earlier noted, occurred in the spring of 1900, when a group of Symiote sponge gatherers set off for home from the waters of North Africa in their two sailing boats. During the journey, bad weather drove them off course and forced them to seek shelter near the small Greek islet of Antikythera, otherwise Cerigotto. While they were thus delayed, Elias Stradiatis, one of the divers, decided to make a routine descent—and promptly returned to the surface with a story of having found himself in the vicinity of a wrecked ship, surrounded by jumbled heaps of bronze and marble figures, scattered over the sea-bed. And by way of proof, he brought with him an outsize metal arm.

The discoverer and his captain, Demetrios Kondos, reported the find to the authorities in Athens, who at once engaged the divers to recover what they could from the wreck, and placed a vessel of the Hellenic Navy, equipped with heavy lifting gear, at their disposal. The task of recovery began in late November, and went on for the next nine months, slowed down by storms and by the depth of 150 feet or more (which restricted each diver to a working time of five minutes, not more than twice daily), and constantly interrupted by accidents (in which one man died, and two others were permanently disabled by the bends).

The recovered items, when they came to be examined, were evidently works of art plundered from Greece, and the collection proved to be a mixture of the good and the bad, the latter predominating. There were, however, a number of bronze figures, some with their leaden bases misshapen and bent, exactly as they had appeared when torn from their pedestals, of which two were considered to be originals of singular merit. Of these presumed representatives of the Periclean Age, one, depicting a youthful athlete, has since been attributed to the famed artist Lysippos. But for the rest, the raiders, it seemed, had shown little discrimination in their stealing. Whereas some of the bronzes had been up to 400 years old at the time of their seizure, the much more numerous marbles (which in any event had been badly corroded by molluscs) proved to be inferior copies of recent manufacture.

Many minor objects, evidently furnishings from the wrecked ship itself, were also brought to the surface, among them a gold earring, a lamp, several amphorae, cooking pots, and some glass vessels. But at once the most interesting and unexpected find was a bronze mechanism, at first thought to be the earliest known representation of an astrolabe. But when, in later years, Derek de Solla Price, an expert on the history of scientific instruments, came to examine the device, with its complex system of gear-trains and slip rings, and its dials showing the annual motion of the sun in the zodiac and the risings and settings of the stars, he pronounced it to be an astronomical clock, in the form of a digital computer!

Seven years after the Antikythera incident, Greek sponge divers happened upon yet another heavily laden Roman plunder ship. On this occasion, the remains of the vessel were found in Tunisian waters, three miles offshore from the small Arab town of Mahdia. The wreck lay at a depth of 130 feet, its presence indicated by a cargo of more than half a hundred fluted marble columns, in the company of a confusion of amphorae, statues, furniture, vases, and the like. Prompted by visions of private gain, the instinctive reaction of the finders was to purloin what they could. And no less predictably (cf. events in Egypt), immediately they attempted to dispose of their unique and priceless booty, word of it reached the authorities, who promptly intervened.

At the time, the Director of Antiquities in Tunis was Alfred Merlin, a Frenchman, who soon became aware that a number of unusual and rare art items, apparently genuine, were on sale in the local bazaars. Diligent enquiries traced the objects to their underwater source, notwithstanding the totally unexpected nature of which, it was decided to attempt to raise the cargo in its entirety. Merlin was able to obtain the assistance of the French Navy, and thanks to the interest in the enterprise shown by his influential friend Salomon Reinach, generous contributions of money were forthcoming from rich patrons of the arts, prominent amongst whom was James Hazen Hyde, an American millionaire then resident in Paris.* Additional funds were provided by the Tunisian Government and a number of French institutions, and one way and another sufficient cash was raised to finance the work of recovery for the next five seasons (1908–13).

In the course of lifting some of the columns, the divers came upon a collection of artistic masterpieces sufficiently numerous

---

*J. Y. Cousteau[34] has recounted how, on the occasion of a visit to New York in 1952, he chanced to meet this particular benefactor, who invited him to dinner. Hyde then confessed: 'I've never seen the things that were brought up. In those days one had a lot of money and a steam yacht. I was cruising in the Aegean while they were diving. I never got to the museum at Tunis. Salomon Reinach sent me photographs of the *kraters* and statues. I got a nice letter from Merlin, and the Bey of Tunis gave me a decoration.'

to fill five galleries of the Alaoui Museum at Bardo, Tunis. Works in marble included a bust of Aphrodite, a Pan, and two Niobids, while among many bronze items, in addition to huge *kraters* and candelabra, were a magnificent statue of a winged Eros and a head of Dionysius, both bearing the signature of the sculptor Böethos the Chalcedonian.

From the evidence available, it was concluded that, like its companion in misfortune found off Antikythera, the Mahdia vessel had gone down in a storm in the first half of the first century B.C., and that it may have contained loot from Athens gathered by Lucius Cornelius Sulla after his sacking of that town in 86 B.C. But if this were the case, why was the ship so far off course, assuming it to have been bound for Italy? Again, if it were a plunder ship, why had it been so overloaded with comparatively valueless columns, estimated to weigh some 200 tons?

What has been held to be a more probable explanation of the nature of the ship's cargo and its destination suggests that the vessel was carrying a pre-fabricated Roman temple and its furniture, made in Greece (where craftsmen abounded) for transportation and erection in North Africa (where skilled artisans were scarce). This ingenious theory would at any rate help to explain why so much of the cargo space was taken up, in addition to the aforementioned columns, by capitals, plinths, and horizontal members of the Ionic Order, together with a complete, if small, marble building.

Two subsequent underwater discoveries, though they also resulted in the recovery of original works of Greek art, concerned isolated examples. In 1925, fishermen casting their nets in the Bay of Marathon brought up the bronze statue of a youth, which examination showed to be an outstanding piece of sculpture, in the style of Praxiteles. The bronze base of a candelabrum was also raised, but although the existence of a promising wreck thus appeared to be indicated, it has yet to be found, though not for the want of trying. Meanwhile, in the year following the Marathon episode, fishermen operating off Cape Artemision, at the southern point of Euobea, brought up a massive bronze arm. Apparently, the finders then made discreet approaches to the antiquarians of Athens, as a result of which it was arranged that the gentlemen concerned would

22. Head of the massive bronze statue of Poseidon, recovered from the sea in the vicinity of Cape Artemision in 1926 (from a photograph).

finance the recovery of the main body of the figure. This was, in fact, located in the course of the next two years, during which, however, the authorities had learned what was afoot in time for them to step in and confiscate the prize. It proved to be a magnificent work, dated about 450 B.C., which has been as-cribed to Kalamis, a contemporary of Myron. At first the statue was held to be a figure of Zeus in anger, brandishing a missing thunderbolt, but it is now considered that the open fingers of the right hand in all probability once grasped a trident, which would identify the deity as Poseidon.

George Karo, of the German Archaeological Institute in Athens, organized an expedition to search the area where the statue was discovered, and with the co-operation of the Greek Navy and a group of sponge divers, the wreck of a ship was located at a depth of 150 feet. Also found were the bronze figure of a boy rider ('The Jockey of Artemision') and fragments of his horse. But at this interesting point, work at the site came to an end, in part because of a lack of funds, but also because of the death of one of the participants. The sponge gatherers, accustomed to working in much shallower waters, were never-theless scornful of the need to decompress on their return from the depths, and the tragedy occurred when one of their number disdainfully shot to the surface at high speed, clambered aboard the support vessel, and laughingly proved his point by dropping dead from an embolism.

By this time, attention had been drawn to what appeared to be the site of an ancient wreck in the vicinity of Albenga, a town on the Italian Riviera. At a distance of some 1,600 yards from the shore, from a depth of 130 feet, local fishermen periodically dragged up Roman amphorae in their nets—first in 1925, then in 1930, and again during the period 1945–7. The presence of a sunken cargo ship was soon thereafter confirmed, and its position established, whereupon Nino Lamboglia, Director of the *Instuto Internazionale di Study Liguri*, at Bordighera, applied for governmental aid, that he might undertake an official investigation of the site. On it being learned that no public funds were available, attempts were then made to interest a group of amateur divers in the project, but at the time, their interests were restricted to shooting fish and searching for treasure. In these circumstances, when an offer of assistance came from the well-known marine salvage firm of Sorima (Società Ricuperi Marittima) of Genoa, Nino Lamboglia was in no mood to decline, and in February, 1950, the firm's salvage vessel *Artiglio II* arrived and moved into position. After the site had been examined by helmeted divers and a few amphorae raised by hand, the method adopted was to bite into the wreck and its cargo of jars with an outsize mechanical grab, whose movements were controlled from an underwater observation chamber by an occupant who was in telephonic communication with the surface. This drastic treatment was continued

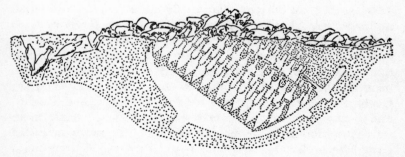

23. *Sectional representation of the ancient Roman amphora carrier wrecked off Albenga. Italy (after Nino Lamboglia).*

for ten days, at the end of which an estimated 1,200 amphorae had been recovered, as many as 110 of them in one piece. Such was the standard of deep water archaeological excavation which prevailed up to the middle of the twentieth century!

It should in fairness be added that under Nino Lamboglia a much more responsible investigation of the site was subsequently undertaken, and that the work has since continued.* After a group of free divers had failed to find the vessel in April, 1957, two members of the team (Alessandro Pederzini and Gianni Roghi), of the *Centro Italiano di Ricercatori Subacquei*, based at Genoa) succeeded in locating it during November of the same year, when a preliminary survey was made and a plan prepared. The wreck lay, partly buried, on a level stretch of sand and mud, broadside-on to the coast with its bows pointing due north. The remains, at their highest point, stood about two yards above the sea-floor, while towards the stern end of the burial mound, running across its full width, was a deep cleft which exposed the lower layers of its tightly packed cargo. Concerning the extent of this man-made gash, it was afterwards reported:

> From the exploration made by us, we can affirm that the wreck has not, in fact, been mangled by the work of the *Artiglio II*, and particularly by the grab, as has often been said and written by people who have never seen it.

Nevertheless, as is now generally conceded, the Sorima incident was an unfortunate mistake, not to be repeated. Meanwhile, as if to make amends for their earlier lack of interest, the authorities placed the *Diano*, an ex-German minesweeper, at the disposal of the *Centro Sperimentale di Archeologia Sottomarina* of Albenga, which Nino Lamboglia had founded in 1958. Thanks to this initiative, and to the organization's possession of a well equipped support vessel, not to mention the close co-operation of the C.I.R.S. divers from Genoa (notably in the persons of Drs. Pederzini and Roghi), underwater research in Italy was placed on a much more satisfactory footing. The maiden mission of the newly acquired *Diano* was undertaken in June, 1959, when those attending a

---

*Published accounts of these activities, well illustrated with photographs and diagrams, will be found in *Forma Maris Antiqui II*, 1959, and subsequent issues.

First Experimental Course in Underwater Archaeology visited the vicinity of the Albenga site and took part in a surface exercise designed to locate and fix the position of the wreck with the aid of an ultrasonic scanner, used in conjunction with other navigational instruments.

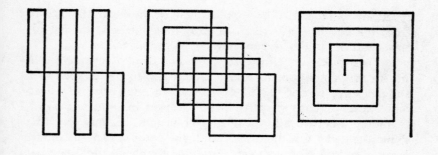

Chapter Five

Men, Methods and Materials

I

Given that, throughout their useful life, major items of archaeological interest now lying under water may be classified as
either mobile or non-mobile, it will be apparent that the
remains of the one promise to be less easy to find than those of
the other. Thus the existence, if not the precise location, of an
immovable structure such as a harbour installation or a group
of drowned villas, is likely to be a matter of record. Again, the
purposeful submergence involved in laying the foundations of
port facilities, no less than the unforeseen inundation of
dwelling places, implies a coastal (or a lakeside) environment,
which in turn suggests the probability of a relatively shallow
immersion. And in these favourable circumstances, the outlines
of a brick or stone edifice, even if its exact whereabouts are
unknown, should not be too difficult to trace—particularly if
there is resort to photographic methods of reconnaisance, a
procedure originally applied to the detection of otherwise
unobservable sites on dry land. Both the arduous journeyings of
J. L. Burckhardt among the mountains of Edom (in his search
for the rock-hewn stronghold of Petra) and the extensive
wanderings of A. H. Mouhot in the jungles of Cambodia (which
eventually brought him to the ruins of the long-lost city of
Angkor Thom) could largely have been avoided if, instead of
conducting their explorations on foot, or at any rate at ground

level, the two men had been able to make a survey of the terrain from the air, in the manner of Antione Poidebard during his investigations of the ancient ports of Tyre and Sidon.

By contrast, the effectiveness of aerial photography as a means of spotting an isolated, random-placed object such as a sunken ship, resting, as likely as not, in comparatively deep water and perhaps more than half buried in mud and sand, or hidden beneath a forest of marine vegetation, has yet to be demonstrated.* On the other hand, the camera can, of course, be used to take close-up pictures *in situ*, thanks to the successful outcome of attempts to engage in underwater photography which have now been going on for many decades. Promising results first appear to have been achieved by Louis Boutan[14] as early as 1893, and by the turn of the century, with the aid of artificial lighting, he had demonstrated an ability to take pictures at a depth of 165 feet, and had published a treatise on various aspects of the undertaking, including the subject of marine optics.

His work was taken up in America, and in 1914 John E. Williamson produced the first undersea film, shot from a submerged cabin attached to the underside of the boat which served as his floating headquarters. The making of coloured photographs soon followed (W. H. Longley, 1923), as did an attempt to transmit underwater television pictures (H. Hartman, 1925), this last an enterprise which heralded a viewing technique subsequently employed by the U.S. Navy in 1947 to examine the effects of the atomic bomb test carried out at Bikini in that year. The first use of television cameras to locate a sunken vessel (H.M. submarine *Affray*) came in 1951,

---

*Some little time ago the American Space Agency drew attention to the means available for a rapid scanning of the oceans of the world by earth satellites, as a result of which, at a conference sponsored by the Oceanographic Institution at Woods Hole, Massachusetts, in August, 1964, consideration was given to 'The Feasibility of Conducting Oceanographic Explorations from Aircraft, Manned Orbital and Lunar Laboratories'.

More recently, in answer to a query about possible archaeological implications, the author received the following reply from W. E. Berg, of the National Aeronautics and Space Council (private communication, 22 October 1969):

While the potential for space photography is great for oceanography as indicated by the pictures obtained to date, I do not recall having seen any photographs that might reveal details of interest to marine archaeology. This, however, should not be considered as ruling out such possibilities in the future. Undoubtedly, an important element in making such a judgement is the trained eye of marine archaeologists. Insofar as I know, no such critical examination has been made.

and in 1954, by the same means, Royal Navy technicians succeeded in finding vital parts of the widely scattered wreckage of the Comet airliner *Yoke Peter*, at an operational depth of 600 feet.

Nor does the eye of the camera provide the only means of scanning the ocean floor, for it is also possible to obtain an acoustic profile of the sea bed (and of any objects resting on it) by means of an echo-sounder. This apparatus, in its various forms, is a lineal descendant of the hydrophones used during World War I in an attempt to detect the presence of enemy submarines. In the event, a satisfactory answer to the problem was not forthcoming until after hostilities had ended, when, with the co-operation of the French, the British Navy's 'Asdic' device was developed.* In operation, a directional supersonic wave is sent out under water, and received back as an echo from the sea bottom—or from the hull of an intervening submarine or other object. The incoming signals, after amplification, are sent to a recorder, consisting essentially of a pen which moves over a sheet of graph paper marked off in metres. The extent of the movement is proportional to the depth, and since the velocity of sound in water of varying degrees of temperature and salinity is known, the echo provides an accurate and continuous outline of the contours of the sea bed as the ship sails over it.

Of more specialized use, and of particular value in indicating the presence of buried metallic objects, are various types of detecting equipment. In its conventional form (available as a self-contained portable model), the metal detector has a range of about 10 feet, while the more intricate magnetometer, an instrument which reacts to distortions in the earth's magnetic field, can operate over a much greater distance. In so far as the underwater archaeologist is concerned, however, the proposed use of such devices is attended by certain difficulties and limitations, not the least of which is the question of cost. Highly sophisticated instrumentation tends to be expensive to buy and install, and (since this requires trained personnel) to maintain and use. Its employment, moreover, imposes very precise

*The term 'Asdic' (derived from Allied Submarine Detection Investigation Committee) was replaced in 1963 by its American equivalent 'Sonar' (SOund NAvigation and Ranging).

navigational requirements as the support vessel makes its way back and forth over the designated area of search. There are also operational problems to be taken into account. Thus metal detectors do not distinguish between an old and valuable artifact and a piece of modern, worthless scrap, and neither does the magnetometer, whose reliability is liable to be upset by unevenness of the ground. The readings it gives can also be misleading in other ways, e.g., it tends to equate a strong influence from a distance with a weak one from nearby. Similarly, in the absence of still water and a more or less flat terrain, neither the echo-sounder nor the television camera can be relied upon to provide an instantly recognizable image of a wreck-containing tumulus, though viewers may be granted a tantalizing glimpse of likely looking mounds which merit a closer inspection by divers. But in these circumstances, those called upon to make a succession of individual investigations would be more usefully employed if they remained submerged and conducted the search in person—and this, in the past, has been the customary procedure.

II

An extended search, however, entails a considerable amount of exertion on the part of a swimmer, and this is undesirable in an undertaking which relies upon human endurance, itself subject to a strict depth-time ratio. Perhaps the ultimate answer, at any rate in so far as a preliminary survey of a particular region is concerned, is to be found in the miniature, two-man submarine devised and built by members of the *Office Français de Recherches Sous-Marines*. In this enterprise, the O.F.R.S. (which J. Y. Cousteau founded in 1952) received financial and other backing from a number of interested organizations, including the influential National Geographic Society.

The vessel took the form of a disc-shaped object, variously nicknamed the Diving or Flying Saucer. It was built to attain and withstand the pressure to be encountered at a depth of 1,500 feet, and was specifically designed for the purpose of exploring the continental shelf. On completion, it emerged with viewing ports, externally located cameras (both still and movie) with associated lighting systems, and was fitted with hydraulic

20. The "Youth of Marathon", a bronze original in the style of
Praxiteles, recovered from the sea in 1925. It stands 4 feet 3 inches
high and is dated 350 B.C. (Photo: *The National Archaeological
Museum, Athens*)

21, 22. Bronze statues recovered from the sea off Cape Artemision (North Euboea) in the late 1920s. (*Above*) Poseidon, attributed to Kalamis, *c.* 450 B.C.; (*below*) the Jockey (second century B.C.), part of a figure of a young rider astride a galloping horse (which is missing). Note the spurs, attached to the heels with thongs. (Photos: *The National Archaeological Museum, Athens*)

24. Submarine scooter, propelled by a battery-driven electric motor (from a photograph).

grabs for the acquisition of specimens. Propulsion, by water jets, enabled the boat to move in any direction, or merely to hover, as its occupants chose. And they, safe within their pressurized compartment, suffered neither fatigue nor the inconveniences of decompression procedures on returning to the surface.

But such immunity is only to be had at a price which not all archaeological expeditions are able to afford, especially as divers will still be needed to visit and make an on-the-spot examination of any prospective sites that may be discovered. Accordingly, a much less expensive Cousteauvian aid to underwater locomotion has been provided in the guise of a submarine scooter, a torpedo-shaped mechanism propelled by a one horse power electric motor driven by 24-volt batteries, a combination capable of delivering a 28-pound thrust for a period of two hours. In use, the driver grasps a handlebar with both hands, his right hand controlling both starter and throttle merely by squeezing. Thus equipped, a diver is enabled to skim far over the sea floor without effort at a speed of about 3 knots.

Objections to the use of the scooter in an underwater search have been raised on a number of grounds. There is, for example, the question of the rider's lack of bodily movement (which ordinarily helps to keep him warm) in a rush of water which likewise serves to deprive him of bodily heat. Exception, too, has been taken to what is regarded as the excessive speed of the vehicle (though this could surely be adjusted), as it represents about the maximum that is permissible if, in the absence of a protective shield, mask and mouthpiece are not to be swept off the driver's face. This is a prospect, incidentally, which promises to restrict activities in tidal waters, where an attempt to go against the stream could give rise to a stationary situation in which progress was nullified by the flow of the current.

The extent of the scooter rider's ability accurately to follow a pre-determined course has also been questioned. Over a wide and flat expanse of territory, devoid of distinguishing landmarks, it is argued that all sense of direction would be lost, or that at best the course chosen would be the result of guesswork in the absence of navigational aids. On the other hand, if the machine were to be fitted with the necessary instruments, an operator who paid due heed to them would have small opportunity to take note of his surroundings—the ostensible purpose of the exercise. In the light of such criticisms, many divers prefer to revert to the simplicity of the towing boat procedure, in which the observer clings to a sled attached to a rope, or merely to a weighted line, and is thereby relieved of the onus of steering.

In such an arrangement, the responsibility for maintaining direction is transferred to the captain of the towing vessel, and

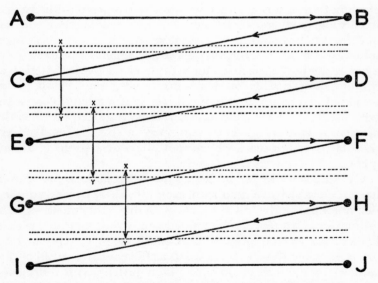

25. In the search pattern here shown (see text for detailed description), the parallel lines AB, CD, EF, GH . . . provide a series of overlapping courses, whose width apart is governed by the distance x–y, representing the limit of underwater visibility.

he, in conducting the search, may adopt one of a number of procedures, such as that which involves him in the making of a series of parallel courses whose distance apart is governed by the clarity of the water. The first step is to buoy a rectangular area, ABCD, in which the lines AB and CD represent the long sides of the enclosure, and the width, as indicated by AC and BD, is less than the underwater visibility distance, thus allowing for overlap. The ship, after moving from A to B, then sails diagonally from B to C, so reaching the starting point of the next parallel course which runs from C to D. When this has been accomplished, the marker at C is moved along the line AC to a new position E, it being ensured that the dimension $AC=CE$ (i.e., $AE=2AC=2CE$). After the diagonal DE has been followed and the line BD has been extended to a point F ($BD=DF$), the observer can then be towed along the parallel EF, and the sequence of operations repeated as often as necessary.

There are many variants of the above procedure, including those intended for use by untowed swimmers and involving search patterns designed to cover relatively small areas which may be oblong, square, or circular in shape, as the conditions prevailing dictate. The much greater cover which the towed system makes possible has also been achieved by linking a dozen or more swimmers in a straight line, along which they are spaced at a distance apart somewhat less than twice that which underwater visibility allows. In action, the whole line moves forward across the full width of one buoyed area after another, guided by a centrally located controller who can be directed, if need be, by an observer at the surface.

But despite the rigorous application of such methods, not even the locating of a well established wreck whose whereabouts have been more or less accurately charted can be regarded as a foregone conclusion, as members of the G.E.R.S. discovered when they paid a visit to Mahdia in 1948.

III

At this time, the G.E.R.S. (*Groupe d'Etude et de Recherches Sous-Marines*), an organization founded at the instigation of J. Y. Cousteau under the aegis of the French naval authorities at

Toulon, had been in existence for three years. To begin with, the group had no more than a couple of launches at its disposal, but to these there was later added a captured German ocean-going tender, a gift from the Ministry of Marine, which was re-named *L'Ingénieur Élie Monnier*, in memory of a deceased comrade. And it was on board this vessel that a team of G.E.R.S. divers, with Cousteau and Tailliez at their head, in due course found themselves anchored in Tunisian waters in the vicinity of Carthage, intent upon carrying out exercises designed to test the efficiency of their recently acquired aqua-lungs. While thus engaged, they heard about the much more promising Mahdia site, to which they promptly transferred their attention.

Their first problem was to locate the Roman wreck, though no difficulty was anticipated, in view of the precise details of its position contained in the official archives, to which they had access. The relevant information consisted of drawings of a series of local landmarks, intended to serve as crossbearings. Of these, one depicted an ancient citadel (the Bordy of Mahdia), aligned with the wall of a jetty on the beach. Another showed an isolated bush, in conjunction with the crest of a hill, while a third involved a distant olive grove, displaying a distinctive foliage with a windmill in the foreground. It was quickly discovered, however, that in the course of the years, most of these indications had either vanished, or were no longer recognizable. Enquiries about a mill resulted in native guides leading them to a number of heaps of rubble representative, not of one, but of several such alleged structures, while the lone bush referred to in the instructions had become a forest. After many vain attempts to identify these and other clues, it was eventually decided to search for the wreck on the assumption that its exact location was not known —a realistic assessment which, as one of the group wryly remarked, did not greatly exaggerate the situation.

Thereafter, the undertaking was conducted on the basis (1) that the remains of the ship were somewhere nearby; and (2) that they lay in about 127 feet of water. What was regarded as a likely position, at the requisite depth, was then covered by a wire grid, extending over 100,000 square feet of the sea floor, and each of its sections methodically examined. This exploration alone took two days—and produced a blank. The area of search was accordingly widened, by towing an observer round the perimeter of the grid on an undersea sledge, again without result. Finally, on the morning of the sixth day, Tailliez, who preferred to cling to a line, was taken closer inshore—and indicated that the quest was over by releasing a signal buoy.

In the event, of the six working days that had been allowed for the completion of the operation, no less than five had been spent in a frustrating search for the remains of the vessel—all because, when at last these were found, their supposed position (as determined by a trio of crossbearings taken several decades earlier) proved to be more than 200 yards out!*

Cousteau, accompanied by Dumas, went down to make a preliminary investigation of the site which, though unrecognizable as a ship, was outlined by its cargo of columns, occupying an area 130 feet long and some 40 feet wide. An attempt at salvage was decided upon, a task which was assisted by the use of a special set of diving tables, prepared for the occasion. They were designed to enable the divers to undertake a series of brief descents, thereby reducing the danger of nitrogen narcosis to a minimum, and calling for no more than a short decompression stop on the return to the surface, and this only on the occasion of the third dive of the day. The procedure depended for its success upon a strict adherence to a rigid time table, and those below were kept audibly informed of the chronological situation by a rifleman on deck, who fired into the water at five minute intervals!

After several of the columns had been raised from a position amidships, debris covering the area thus left exposed was removed by means of a high pressure water jet, and at a depth of two feet or thereabouts deck timber was encountered. This proved to be solid and undamaged, and offered a barrier beneath which, it was considered, there might well exist an intact cargo awaiting a finder, though this inviting possibility was one which the G.E.R.S. divers did not have the time to investigate. Instead, they contented themselves with the few

*Five years later, members of the local *Club d'Etude Sous-Marines*, based at Tunis also decided to take a look at the site. But although they had the benefit of the experience of their G.E.R.S. predecessors, and employed the same towing and sweeping techniques, assisted in addition by sonar and other devices, the wreck continued to elude them until a second attempt to find it was made in the following year!

columns they had already retrieved, together with sundry other items which included anchor parts and pieces of varnished Lebanon cedar from the ship itself.

While these activities were in progress, a heap of amphorae was discovered off Anthéor Point, near Cannes—all that was visible of what proved to be the remains of another sunken ship and its freight dating from the first century B.C. The site was covered with concretion and was overgrown with poseidon grass, and a great deal of effort was expended by its finders in clearing it. The *Élie Monnier* reached the scene in the following year, and returned in 1950, with equipment designed to speed the task of burrowing into the tightly packed cargo. To this end, the visitors introduced a powerful *suceuse*, or suction hose. Among divers, this device was soon to establish itself as a multi-purpose excavational tool, invented, according to Philippe Tailliez,[133] at G.E.R.S. headquarters, where it had been perfected in 1946. But the fact is, as Frédéric Dumas[50] has been at some pains to show, that the history of the emulsion pump (as it is also known) may be traced, by way of scores of published references and specifications, as far back as the end of the eighteenth century, to the person of one Carl Immanuel Löscher (*Erfindung eines Aerostatischen Kunstgezeuges*, Leipzig, 1797). To the Cousteau team, however, must go the credit for adapting and introducing the so-called air-lift to the excavational needs of underwater archaeology.

In its essentials, the device merely consists of a rigid tube of uniform diameter, with an inlet pipe near one extremity to which is attached a length of hose, which in turn is connected to a compressor or other source of pressurized air. When such a tube is immersed vertically in water, in such a manner that its upper end projects above the surface (though not to an unlimited extent), and air is pumped into its lower extremity, streams of bubbles rush upwards, increasing in size and gathering speed all the while, in the process giving rise to a powerful suction action. As a result, water, sand, mud, pebbles and other small objects in the vicinity of the mouth of the tube are drawn into it and carried aloft with considerable force.

It will be evident that the supply of air needs to be at a pressure which exceeds that of the surrounding water at inlet level, and that, in consequence, the deeper the submergence, the more powerful will be the lifting action that is produced. Again, the speed of the ascending bubbles is governed by the diameter of the tube, optimum sizes ranging from 3 to 6 inches, and varying in accordance with the individual circumstances of a particular site. Maximum output occurs at surface level, beyond which, as the upper end of the tube is raised more and more above the water, there is a steady decrease in the rate of discharge, which finally ceases altogether. Fortunately, this critical height (which varies in accordance with tube characteristics) is of small concern to the archaeologist, as it is normally not exceeded by his working requirements. Indeed, as will later be seen, there are occasions when it is advantageous for the discharge to take place below the surface, usually into a wire basket which retains all items of possible interest.

The air-lift is to be regarded as indispensable when it comes to the removal of the vast quantities of sand (amounting to several hundred tons) which the excavation of a ship may be expected to entail. But its indiscriminate use for the uncovering (and even raising) of artifacts is not to be recommended, as it so often entails their destruction or damage, quite apart from stratigraphical and allied considerations. After an initial period of over-exuberant employment by members of the diving fraternity, self-imposed restrictions soon came to be placed upon its use. At the same time, and in the light of this same operational experience, various improvements were made to the instrument itself, including the addition of flexible extremities to the ends of the tube; the attaching of one or more handles to assist its manipulation underwater; and the affixing of a hinged rubber ring at the intake, as a means of ensuring the easy removal of objects causing a blockage.

Though in action the reverse of the air-lift, the high pressure water jet has also found extensive use in submarine excavation, and it, too, has been modified in a manner dictated by its fluid surroundings. To counteract the tendency of the hose to react violently when in operation, Arne Zetterström devised a jet in which the recoil was nullified by a series of minor escape vents pointing in the opposite direction. Nozzles of this type were employed to excavate the six tunnels in the mud under the *Vasa*, in preparation for the lifting of that vessel, and they were used, moreover, in conjunction with airlifts, which sucked up and carried away the clouds of sediment to which the operation gave rise.

IV

No sooner had G.E.R.S. members completed their investigations at Anthéor Point than information was received about the existence of an as yet untouched site which Cousteau and his colleagues were destined to make their own. It appeared that the wreck of a large amphora carrier was to be found near one of a chain of barren limestone islets situated some ten miles from Marseilles. The archipelago was the favourite haunt of a lobster gatherer by the name of Gaston Christianini who, in the course of his diving activities, suffered a severe attack of the bends. He was rushed to the naval station at Toulon for treatment, in the course of receiving which he encountered Frédéric Dumas, to whom, during his convalescence, he spoke at length about his experiences. It was during these discussions that mention was made of the small island of Grand Congloué, and of some of its distinctive underwater features, one in the form of a vast natural arch, etched in the submerged rock face of the island at a depth of 100 feet, and another in the shape of a mass of old jars, lying in a tumbled heap on the floor of the sea. . . .

According to Yves Girault,[134] the site of the wreck had earlier been noticed by helmeted divers engaged in the construction of a new Marseilles sewer, the outlet of which lay almost opposite Grand Congloué. However, these men did not attach any importance to the sight of a few old pots strewn on the sea-bed, and it remained for Frédéric Dumas to realize their significance. So it came about that Cousteau, absent on a shakedown trip to the Red Sea in a newly acquired research ship, the *Calypso*, learned about Grand Congloué on his return. And early in 1952, in the course of a conference held on board the vessel, at which Fernand Benoit, the Director of Antiquities for Provence and Corsica, was present, the decision was taken to investigate the fisherman's story—which proved to be reliable. On sloping ground at the base of a steep cliff, at a depth which increased from 125 to 140 feet, the searchers came upon a large tumulus from whose summit there protruded an array of amphora necks, in the company of some broken pottery. The mound was some 135 feet in length and about 36 feet wide, and was later estimated to contain as many as 10,000 jars. This was an unexpectedly heavy load, for when planning the expedition, a period of eight weeks had been allowed in which to complete the investigation. In the event, the task was still unfinished at the end of eight years. . . .

In the course of centuries, large pieces of rock had detached themselves from the cliff above and dropped onto the wreck, though without crushing it, as the water had cushioned their fall. The first job was to clear the site of this and other debris, though one outsize boulder, weighing many tons, was removed only after it had been split into several large fragments with the aid of an explosive charge, by which time something of the size and extent of the undertaking had become evident, and the need for outside assistance realized. Thanks to the publicity the enterprise had already received, help was at once forthcoming in the shape of men, money, and materials. Volunteer divers offered their services from all over France, ministerial and other bodies (including the ubiquitous National Geographic Society) provided financial aid, and when, in the face of increasingly unsettled weather which threatened the safety of *Calypso*, it was considered prudent to conduct operations from a base camp on the island, Army engineers blasted a platform in the rock face, and affixed a steel ladder which gave access to a stretch of sloping ground at a higher level, upon which Nissen huts were erected. These living quarters were then furnished by the civic authorities and the Marseilles Chamber of Commerce, who also provided additional equipment which included such useful items as a refrigerator, an electric light plant, and two-way radio-telephone facilities.

Down below, the site of the wreck was marked by four submerged buoys, within the area of which as many as sixteen divers worked in the course of a day, their air supply being provided by the usual portable bottles carried on the back, or by way of a *narghile*.* Two-man teams operated in relays, each

---

*In this arrangement (also known as a *hookah*), air is supplied to the aqualung through a hose connected to a compressor (or other source) at the surface. Provided the diver is not required to move about to any great extent, the inconvenience of the air line is compensated for by the fact that he is untroubled by the need to watch his air consumption. But as George Bass and his associates discovered at Cape Gelidonya (see page 171ff.), when the hoses were used where there was a strong current, the drag on them was so great that descents to, and ascents from, the site

making a maximum of three dives within a twenty-four hour period, respectively of 18, 15, and 12 minutes duration, with a three-to-five minute decompression stop at a depth of ten feet from the surface on the return journey. The signal for their recall, as at Mahdia, was the sound of a rifle shot.

Despite delays and interruptions, the wreck was cleared of obstructions and broken crockery, and some 300 of the amphorae raised. At first the jars, between three and four feet tall, were winched to the surface strung to a line, or bunched together in a cargo net, though not without some breakages. Then one of the divers hit upon the idea of filling an inverted amphora with sufficient air to take it to the surface, though it was soon discovered that cracked specimens displayed a tendency to disintegrate during ascent. Eventually, the problem of safe retrieval was solved by placing the jars in a wire basket, and hoisting them aloft a dozen at a time.

With the removal of the comparatively loosely packed topmost layer of the cargo, there was exposed a solidified mass from which it was no longer possible to extricate the jars merely by tugging at them. Resort was then had to a powerful air-lift, which in addition to dispersing sedimentation, sucked up and conveyed to the collecting basket an assortment of copper nails, pieces of lead sheathing, and bits of timber, a flow of items which continued unabated until one day it was augmented by countless fragments of newly broken pottery, among which was found an exquisite wine cup which had somehow survived its turbulent journey through the pipe. With the belated realization that, injudiciously used, the air-lift in its existing form could become an instrument of wholesale destruction, a reducing nozzle and a grill were added. At the same time, care was taken to ensure that the items of tableware, once they had been extricated from the wreck, were conveyed to the surface in a manner which ensured that they arrived in one piece. As a result, some hundreds of dishes, bowls, drinking cups, and the like were safely recovered, as in due course was a solitary amphora with its seal intact and its original contents uncontaminated by sea water. The container was broached to

---

could be made only with the aid of a climbing line. On occasion, too, kinks developed, cutting off the air supply and forcing two divers to share one mouthpiece.

reveal a transparent, pinkish liquid—red wine that had mellowed for more than 2,000 years. But in the process, alas, it had become completely de-alcoholized, and James Dugan[49] reports that after tasting it, Cousteau declared it to be 'A poor vintage century'.*

While the work of recovery went on, Professor Benoit and his colleagues were kept busy examining and attempting to identify the hundreds—and eventually thousands—of items which the cargo carrier continued to disgorge. Sundry other objects, evidently belonging to the crew, were also recovered, among them an earthenware stove, a heavy marble mortar, and a drinking mug, upon which was scratched, in Greek, the words 'To your health'. Disappointingly, no coins were found, as these would have furnished a firm lower date for the wreck. However, the goods from the vessel's hold and upper deck provided useful information as to this. Thus the pottery, in more than a score of different forms and half a dozen sizes, was Campanian (believed to have emanated from the Naples–Ischia region), and attributable to the first half of the second century B.C. The dating of the amphorae, though it produced a result broadly in agreement with this estimate, was less simple a task, as the jars were of several distinct types which, though mainly Hellenic (lower cargo) and Italic (deck cargo), also included examples of earlier Rhodian and Cnidian ware.†

It had long been noted that many (though by no means all)

---

*The author of this now famous remark unintentionally started a verbal epidemic, for such wit is highly contagious. Thus T. Falcon-Barker[7] has recounted how he and some companions, diving off the Balearic Islands in 1962, discovered a Roman wreck from which a sealed amphora, containing a brackish liquid, was recovered:

We all took a sip. That was as much as anyone was able to swallow—A.D. 50 must have been a bad vintage year!

The jest has even been applied to the product of the distiller of molasses, if Edwin Link has been reported aright. In 1959, during his investigation of the submerged ruins of Port Royal, Link found an unopened bottle of rum. This he sampled, afterwards proclaiming (according to N. C. Flemming[43]) that '1692 must have been a bad year'.

†Since the start of the present century, a typological contribution on the subject by Heinrich Dressel (*Corpus Inscriptionum Latinorum XV*, 1899) has been regarded as the standard work on the identification and dating of amphorae. But Dressel's catalogue was based on incomplete information obtained solely from the excavation of land sites, in particular those of Roman camps along the German frontier (*Limes Germanicus*). In recent years, new discoveries have disclosed important gaps in his system of classification, an arrangement which Fernand Benoit has ventured to simplify and extend in the light of the results of underwater investigations, by the addition of a pre-Roman series, distinguished by the appellation Republican.

amphorae bore epigraphic markings on the lip, shoulder, and stopper, and that these names, assumed to be a reference to the potter, producer, or exporter, were usually in abbreviated form —D (Decimus), Ar (Arilius), Bas (Balbus), and so on. In the present instance, Benoit's curiosity was aroused when he came upon the letters SES on the cap of hundreds of the Italic jars from the wreck, for it so happened that this particular mark had also been encountered (on occasion as the variants SEST, SETS, SESTI) during the excavation of more than a dozen land sites. After considerable genealogical research, he found in the works of Livy a reference to an influential Roman clan named Sestius, a leading member of which, one Marcus

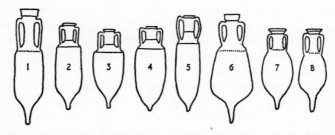

26. *Some of the many amphora types distinguished by Heinrich Dressel in his* Corpus Inscriptionum Latinorum *(1899)*.

Sestius, had established a shipping business on the Greek island of Delos. Moreover, on Delos itself, there was found a stone inscription, dated 240 B.C., recording the fact that Marcus Sestius had been granted Delian citizenship, a signal honour to which the recipient had responded by changing his name to Markos Sestios.

Having regard for the mixed nature of its cargo of amphorae, and of the order of loading, it thus appeared that the Grand Congloué wreck had first acquired a shipment of Greek wine at Delos, and had then called at an Italian port (in all probability Naples) to load deck cargo, before sailing on to a destination which was almost certainly the Phocaean colony of Massalia (the modern Marseilles), near where the vessel was sunk. Nor, in the light of subsequent events, can there be much doubt as to the manner of its end, for on a stormy night in 1953, the

Donatello, an Italian ship from Reggio, carrying a load of turpentine and wax cakes, lost its way in the blinding rain and came to grief on the adjacent islet of Riou—and this notwithstanding that the vessel's captain had at his disposal radar equipment, electric steering, and powerful engines!

V

The amphora carrier at Grand Congloué has been hailed as the first ancient wreck of any consequence, the investigation of which was undertaken from its inception with the aid of modern methods and equipment, notably the aqualung. And as such, it was a pioneer undertaking which necessarily involved much trial and not a little error, as those who were engaged in it

27. *The trade mark of Marcus Sestius, as found on many of the amphorae recovered from the wreck at Grand Congloué.*

freely admit. On the credit side, there was demonstrated, over an extended period of time, the workableness of a deep water site, in the course of which activity novel techniques such as the water jet, the air-lift, submarine illumination, and a system of closed circuit underwater television for observational purposes, were introduced, tested, and improved. And as a salvage operation, it must be acclaimed an outstanding success, having regard for the experimental nature of the enterprise and the results that were obtained in the face of difficult and hazardous conditions (which cost one man his life). But this having been said, it needs to be added that, as an exercise in the niceties of archaeological excavation, it left a great deal to be desired.

   To begin with, the approach to the problem of how to set about the task was ill-conceived—if, indeed, the question was initially given any serious consideration at all. According to Jean Riviore,[87] one of the divers who worked at the site, his instructions were merely 'do what you can within the marked area', and Cousteau[33] himself has conceded that a serious tactical mistake was made at the outset:

> Instead of picking systematically at the upper end, or stern as we called it and working down, we blurred the archaeological picture by gleaning all over the mound.

28. On the floor of a ruined villa on the island of Delos, where Marcus Sestius established his shipping business in the third century B.C., archaeologists uncovered a mosaic which featured a trident with 2 S-shaped brackets between its E-shaped tines, an arrangement reminiscent of the SES with trident marking shown in Fig. 27 above. Is the resemblance which the one insignia bears to the other merely co-incidental, or was the villa the home of Marcus Sestius? (Based on a photograph).

Moreover, some of the methods of retrieval that were employed were highly damaging, not merely to the site as a whole (an unavoidable consequence of excavation), but also to many of the individual artifacts of which it was composed. In later years, after Yves Girault had taken over the task of clearance, Frédéric Dumas,[50] who had worked at Grand Congloué throughout the period of Cousteau's administration, had some scathing comments to make about the manner in which the enterprise was conducted. Under the heading 'Past Mistakes', the relevant passage begins:

When divers, acting as self-appointed archaeologists, first came across groups of amphorae half-buried in the sand, they had no idea of the size of the wreck or its probable depth below the surface. They started to excavate by removing the visible jars then, seeing that there were others, they installed an air-lift to disengage the lower layers. This amounted to no more than the salvage of objects and the result of their efforts was a big hole in the middle of the wreck area . . .

He also drew attention to what he regarded as the imperative need to establish from the start, both the axis of the ship and whether or not it had come to rest on an even keel, that the exact position of the vessel and the full extent of the area over which its cargo had spilled might be determined. This information, he suggested, could readily be obtained by means of a core sampler, an instrument successfully used by oceanographers for a century or more. If it were to be driven into the sea-bed at selected points, it could be relied upon to provide incontrovertible evidence of what lay beneath the covering of mud and sand. But while the effectiveness of such a device in revealing the extent and stratigraphical details of an underwater site is not to be doubted, it would need to be used sparingly and with discretion, if the possibility of causing damage to what might prove to be unique objects was to be avoided. As for the air-lift, Dumas advocated that once the extent of a site has been ascertained, this device might be more usefully (and certainly less destructively) employed to dig a trench round the perimeter of the wreck area. This would serve the double purpose of isolating the wreck at a level higher than that of the surrounding terrain, and so make possible the examination and removal of its cargo layer by layer, instead of by way of a gaping hole with sloping sides.

Other critics have pointed to the scant regard which appears to have been paid to the all-important question of context, i.e., to the placement and association of individual objects, and it would seem that such mapping and recording as was undertaken at Grand Congloué involved little more than the use of a wall

plan, upon which the location of selected finds was noted.
Honor Frost,[60] a professional cartographer with considerable
diving experience, who visited the site in 1960 at the invitation
of Yves Girault, discovered on enquiry that the services of an
underwater draughtsman had at no time been employed—
an omission which has contributed to the continued existence
of certain doubts which have arisen concerning the outcome of
the investigation.

Prior to the work done at Grand Congloué, jars similar to the
Rhodian and Cnidian specimens recovered from the site had
been assigned a date 70 or more years earlier than that of the
rest of the cargo, and Cousteau duly announced the discovery
of amphora types which archaeologists had hitherto attributed
to different ages—the implication here being that the experts
had erred in believing the two items to be other than contemporary. But leading authorities on the subject remained un-
convinced, and even insisted upon the validity of the established
chronology. It is possible, of course, that in addition to a load
of containers of a shape then in vogue, the ship also carried a
consignment of an earlier make and pattern which had
somehow survived a century of wear and tear, and was still in
use. But it has also been conjectured as an alternative and
perhaps more likely explanation, that another vessel had earlier
been wrecked at the same place, and that the superimposed
remains of the two ships were involved—a by no means un-
common situation among the danger spots of the Mediterranean.
Moreover, some substance is lent to this suggestion by the size
of the cargo. Although 10,000 amphora ships are mentioned
by Strabo,[128] vessels of this capacity would appear to have been
exceptional, on account of berthing and other considerations.
It is at all events a matter of record that by Senatorial edict in
218 B.C., the tonnage of merchant ships armed by the Port of
Thasos was limited to 3,000 amphorae. On the other hand, the
divers who worked at Grand Congloué are unanimous in their
rejection of the multiple wreck theory, and what little woodwork
they managed to recover (part of a keel and ribs) clearly came
from a single source, though it has been argued that the exposed
timbers of another ship, lying atop the first, would have long
since disintegrated. It would thus appear that by their failure
to keep detailed records which might have afforded evidence

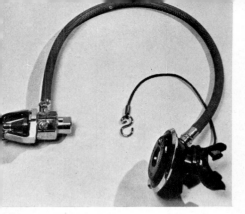

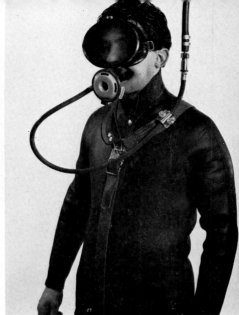

24. Surface demand (narghile) equipment. The Mercury 2 single hose regulator (*above*) incorporates a first stage reducer and a lightweight, mouth-held second stage demand valve. By replacing the first stage reducer with a non-return valve adapter, there results the surface demand equipment shown right. (Photos: *Siebe Gorman*)

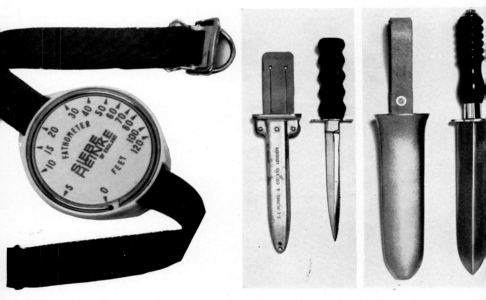

25. Fathometer wrist depth gauge. **26.** Lightweight (*left*) and heavyweight (*right*) underwater knives and sheaths. (Photos: *Siebe Gorman*)

27. Mendel L. Peterson of the Smithsonian Institution, using an azimuth circle and measuring chain to ascertain the range and bearing of parts of an ancient shipwreck in Caribbean waters. (Photo: *The Smithsonian Institution, Washington*)

in support of their contention, Cousteau and his team have left unanswered the question of whether the site marked the grave of one vessel or of two—an unsatisfactory state of affairs which may now remain forever unresolved.

Chapter Six

Divers and Archaeologists

I

Although the existence and whereabouts of scores of ancient wrecks are now known, the fact is that scientific methods had little enough to do with their detection. After the initial discoveries made by net fishermen and sponge gatherers, a succession of other chance finds resulted from the recreational activities of aqualung users, not only in the coastal waters of France, but also in those of Italy and other lands bordering the Mediterranean, where sporting enthusiasts formed associations such as the *Club de la Mer*, at Antibes. Kindred groups were also to be found at Marseilles, St. Raphael, and Juan-les-Pins, while Cannes had its *Club Alpin Sous-Marin*, whose somewhat incongruous title arose from the circumstance that Henri Broussard, its founder, had been a keen mountain climber.

It was Henri Broussard who (in August, 1948) discovered the Anthéor wreck, and as news of the find spread, following the arrival of the G.E.R.S. team aboard the *Élie Monnier*, the site was visited by scores of itinerant divers, most of whom, it soon transpired, came in the guise of souvenir hunters. And inevitably, the fragile framework of the vessel was broken up by the rough treatment it received, so all that now marks the spot are fragments of some of the 2,000 or more storage jars which once made up the cargo.

Such acts of depredation (others soon followed) are essentially a post mid-twentieth century phenomenon. In the days when only the helmeted diving dress was available and in general use,

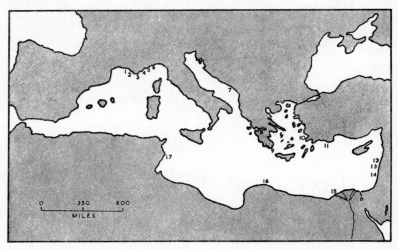

29. *The location of some of the many underwater archaeological sites known to exist in the Mediterranean is shown on the above plan of the region. The numbering follows a clockwise direction: 1, Fos-sur-Mer; 2, Grand Congloué; 3, Titan; 4, Dramont; 5, Anthéor; 6, Albenga; 7, Epidaurus; 8, Helice; 9, Antikythera; 10, Yassi Ada; 11, Cape Gelidonya; 12, Sidon; 13, Tyre; 14, Caesarea; 15, Alexandria; 16, Apollonia; 17, Mahdia.*

possible despoilers were relatively few and their activities not easily conducted in secret. But with the invention and mass production of the inexpensive aqualung, not only did the number of underwater swimmers increase beyond reckoning, but the self-contained nature of the equipment made it virtually impossible for any effective control to be exercised over their movements and activities, legitimate or otherwise. The so-called 'free' diver thus found himself free indeed, able without restraint, were he so minded (or sufficiently mindless) to damage or destroy in a matter of days or weeks an archaeological site which the sea had preserved for thousands of years.

It is true that most, if not all, of the countries directly concerned have introduced legislation designed to ensure the safety and protection of such national heritages. But what the law does not allow, it is not always able to prevent. And although there have been a number of prosecutions concerned with the plundering, or attempted plundering, of ancient wrecks, the great difficulty has always been—and will no doubt continue to be—that of catching the culprits in the act. It is, of course, wholly impracticable to attempt to maintain a constant watch over all the known locations, while in the case of new and unreported finds, there is always the added danger that because of the indiscriminate removal of surface indications, no visible evidence of the existence of a site will remain.

It would seem that the only effective answer to the problem is to be found in the hope of educating would-be offenders, that they may be prevailed upon to abide by an acceptable code of underwater behaviour, the essence of which is simply that if a find is made, its position should be noted and reported, untouched, to someone in authority. The matter is clearly one of increasing urgency, for discoveries continue to be made faster than they can be given the attention they merit, and already enough ancient wrecks have been found to keep accredited investigators fully occupied for many decades to come. It has been suggested that no more searching should be undertaken until the existing back-log of sites has been cleared, but apart from the fact that such an agreement would favour intending vandals (by whom it would be ignored), some chance finds, however unintentional, are bound to keep coming to light, failing an unimposable prohibition of all unauthorized diving activities. In any case, and even if the prospect of early investigation is small, each time another wreck is found it adds to the corpus of information about ancient trade routes and the interchange of goods among peoples, so that new discoveries are to be encouraged if there is any reason to suppose they will be left undisturbed—which brings the discussion back to the question of education.

Fortunately, the various diving clubs early showed a commendable willingness to follow the lead given by the G.E.R.S. of Toulon. As responsible Service divers who were by no means averse to utilizing their skills in the examination of ancient wrecks, its members, once their ambitions became known, received every encouragement and assistance, in particular from Professor Benoit. A policy of close co-operation was agreed upon and maintained, in pursuance of which the Director of Antiquities and his colleagues (as at Grand Congloué) made periodic visits to some chosen scene of operations, there to discuss the work in progress and make a preliminary examination of any finds.

Thus in 1953, Jean Piroux, a medical practitioner from Cannes, was diving off the eastern point of the Île du Levant, in the vicinity of Titan, when at a depth of 93 feet he sighted a cluster of amphorae, outlining the shape of a ship. Piroux re-visited the site in the following year, accompanied by Dimitri Rebikoff, after which Philippe Tailliez, with the approval of Fernand Benoit, sought and obtained permission from the naval authorities for members of the G.E.R.S. to investigate the wreck as part of an official training exercise. But at this juncture, Tailliez was posted abroad, and during his absence he received the unwelcome intelligence that the site had been visited by plunderers, though apparently the culprits had been caught before they could do much damage.

On his return to Toulon in 1957, the planning of the expedition was resumed. It happened that the French Navy owned much of the Île du Levant, on which an experimental station had been established, so that all the essentials of a base camp were immediately available for use by a team of a dozen divers and associated personnel who in due course arrived there. Nor was this the full extent of the expedition's good fortune, for an examination of the site disclosed that the wreck was encircled by protecting walls of rock, wherein it formed an isolated and self-contained unit. The central mound measured some 120 feet long by 36 feet wide, and as a first step, several amphorae were attached to a line and hauled aboard the *Élie Monnier*, where an expectant Benoit at once identified them as belonging to the age of Augustus.

A draughtsman then made a careful survey of the area, from

which drawings were prepared depicting the wreck and the surrounding basin, both in plan and in section. Supplementary information was provided by Tailliez himself, who systematically filmed the site from a fixed height above the sea-bed, so producing a photographic mosaic. Thereafter, by means of a graduated line running approximately due north along one edge of the basin, a similar attention to detail was maintained throughout the excavation. Divers were strictly enjoined, whenever they came upon an object of interest, on no account to disturb it, but merely to determine its position in relation to the base line, and report to the supervisor at the surface. He would then plot the position on a master plan, prior to arranging for the removal of the item.

The divers went down in groups of two or three, the depth concerned permitting a twice daily immersion of 28 minutes, with decompression stops on the occasion of the second return to the surface. The plan of operation not only envisaged the recovery of the entire cargo, but it also called for the clearing and raising of the remains of the ship's hull, to the accompaniment of constant supervision and a continuous recording of the site as the work progressed. As to this, the first task was to dig an exploratory trench from the rim of the rock enclosure to the ship mound, in the course of which an encouraging find was made in the shape of a lead anchor stock.

The trenching was undertaken with the aid of an air-lift, which emptied on to the after-deck of the *Élie Monnier*. Certain limitations associated with this arrangement led to the provision of a floating platform (in the guise of a flat-bottomed boat), fitted with a derrick for lifting or lowering the pipe, which was made up of sections of rubber tube. Thereafter, the flow from the outlet ran into a gutter extending the length of the lighter, by way of a system of screens and baffles through which sedimentary material brought up from the wreck could be filtered.

As the amphorae were uncovered and freed, they were not brought to the surface immediately, but were stacked on one side or other of the central mound, until 500 or so had been accumulated. They were then loaded, 16 at a time, into a basket container, and winched aloft for cleaning and inspection. Meanwhile, among other objects revealed by the air-lift were a corn mill, terracotta lamps, a bronze spoon, and pieces of pottery, until at last bits of worm-eaten wood appeared, soon to be followed by the uncovering of a group of 7 rib members, complete with planking and other remnants of the hull.

Unlike the keel uncovered at Grand Congloué, and also at Mahdia, that of the Titan wreck was doubled by a keelson, into which the ribs, consisting of single crosspieces, had been fitted. As was customary, the lengths of attached planking had been caulked and joined, edge to edge, by tenons dowelled into mortices, a mode of construction which long preceded the overlapping characteristic of clipper-built craft, and one which raises an interesting point: if, during the lifetime of such a vessel, a section of its planking suffered damage, how was it replaced? Up to the time of this writing, the question remains unanswered, and the day is awaited when an archaeologist happens upon a repaired hull. One guess is that it will be found to have been patched.

The surviving woodwork at Titan weighed between two and three tons, its condition so decayed that raising it in one piece proved to be impracticable with the limited means available. The keel was accordingly sawed into two 8-yard lengths, and the attached planking and ribs removed. Each separate piece of the fragile timber was then lashed to an individual support, and carefully brought to the surface, where it was deposited into a barge for transportation to Toulon.

In an account of the undertaking which Tailliez subsequently published (*Travaux de l'été 1958 sur l'épave du 'Titan' à l'île du Levant*, Albenga, 1958), the writer, in acknowledging that many mistakes had been made, laments the lack of expert supervision and advice:

> If we had been assisted from the beginning by an archaeologist, he would surely have noted with much greater accuracy the position of each object; by personal inspection he would have drawn more information from the slightest indications . . .

II

It had by this time become evident that a state of affairs in which the archaeologists did not dive, and the divers were not archaeologists, was an unsatisfactory one in so far as the outcome of a planned excavation was concerned. Predictably, there was a lack of direction and supervision, which in turn led to wrong decisions and procedural errors, with the inevitable result that more than one enterprise which had been begun with high hopes and expectations, soon degenerated into an activity whose main purpose and concern, or so it seemed to outside observers, amounted to little more than the recovery of objects, much of the importance and significance of which was irretrievably lost in the process. What still remains the last authoritative word on such a situation was stated by Flinders Petrie[106] more than sixty years ago:

> To suppose that excavation—one of the affairs which needs the widest knowledge—can be taken up by persons who are ignorant of most or all the technical requirements is a fatuity which has led, and still leads, to the most miserable catastrophes. Far better let things lie a few centuries longer underground, if they can be let alone, than repeat the vandalism of past ages without the excuse of being a barbarian.

Mounting criticism and a questioning of the scientific value of their efforts was not unnaturally resented by members of the diving fraternity, especially as much of the adverse comment came from persons who, however expert they might be in their own chosen field, were without any experience of the many difficulties and hazards which attended work on an underwater site. Nor, after the enterprise and initiative they had shown, did divers take kindly to the suggestion that the time had arrived for them to hand over to those professional archaeologists who had hitherto displayed so little interest in the undertaking. Also taken amiss was the assumption, implicit in the proposed relinquishment, what whereas divers could hardly be expected to succeed as archaeologists, there was no valid reason why archaeologists should not readily attain a high degree of proficiency as divers. Philippe Tailliez,[133] no doubt after comparing his own long and arduous apprenticeship as an underwater swimmer with the relatively short time (usually no more than two months) an archaeologist finds himself able to devote to work in the field each year, went so far as to declare:

> Underwater excavation is a problem for sailors and divers rather than archaeologists.

With this assertion, no practising archaeologist could possibly agree, however willingly he might be prepared to concede the need to draw upon the knowledge and experience of others in what he regarded as primarily maritime matters. And there was a growing conviction, at any rate among the younger members of the profession, that steps must be taken to dispel the sciolistic image of the enterprise reflected in the words of James Dugan:[48]

> In a way, marine archaeology is a science founded without scientists. The initiative for the first Underwater Archaeology Conference held at Cannes in 1955 came from amateurs . . .

30. Obverse and reverse sides of the medallion struck to commemorate the Third International Underwater Archaeological Conference, held in Barcelona in 1961.

The amateurs in question were Henri Broussard and his fellow members of the *Club Alpin Sous-Marin*. And it was at the gathering thus promoted that the long delayed confrontation between divers and archaeologists at last took place.* Nor, by the time the proceedings had ended, could there be any doubt as to the outcome of the encounter, in the course of which Italy's Nino Lamboglia, mindful, no doubt, of the early Albenga episode, insisted upon 'the absolute priority of the archaeological over the technical factor in underwater exploration'.

Ten years later, in a retrospective Foreword to a collective

---

*These international gatherings have since been continued at more or less regular intervals. The second Conference was held at Albenga (Italy) in 1958; the third at Barcelona (Spain) in 1961; and the fourth at Nice (France) in 1970.

work edited by Joan du Plat Taylor,[134] of London University's Institute of Archaeology, a seemingly still somewhat aggrieved J. Y. Cousteau summed up the position thus:

> With the advent of the free-diver, ancient wrecks have been located almost everywhere, rarely properly exploited, though sometimes pillaged. The invasion of the sea by thousands of divers has brought an unhoped for 'census' of sites, but has at the same time struck terror into the archaeologist. This fear is theoretically justified, but it is in fact only a proof of how far the archaeologist lags behind the diver. It is now up to the governments concerned to prevent the development of a serious conflict: legislation must be amended and scientific departments enlarged and given larger sums for excavation. Not a day should be lost. Divers, whose good faith is unquestioned, refuse to be scapegoats and take the responsibility for the defects of the ministries . . .

III

At the Cannes Conference, meanwhile, Professor Lamboglia not only asserted the need for a professional approach to underwater archaeology, but he also drew attention to some of the problems this could be expected to involve. And to these anticipated difficulties he sought an answer by posing a number of questions, here paraphrased in their order of presentation:

1. Was it possible to organize and undertake an underwater excavation with the same attention to detail as on land, and at a comparable cost?

2. For archaeological purposes and needs, was the helmeted dress preferable to the equipment of the free diver?

3. How was control of the undertaking to be exercised by the archaeologist, and what should be his relationship with divers and other technicians?

4. Once the external details of a sunken vessel had been examined and recorded, could excavation then proceed as on land, even to the extent of making a stratigraphical approach?

5. Would available techniques permit the reclamation of an ancient wreck, and, if so, at what cost?

Of the various points contained in this enumeration, that raised by the second item had already been decided (and would presumably not have found mention, had the questioner been familiar at the time with the many advantages the aqualung had to offer), while most of the other issues have since been satisfactorily resolved, as will emerge in the pages which follow. Thus the organizing of an underwater archaeological venture may be expected to conform with established procedure—what promises to be an interesting site is discovered, and its investigation proposed; arrangements to excavate it are made with the owner, and financial backing for the undertaking is sought; both these needs having satisfactorily been met, expedition members are recruited and equipment is assembled; thereafter, men and materials are transported to the site and a base camp (or a maritime equivalent) is established.

The least protracted of these preliminaries is likely to be the making of the initial decision to carry out the investigation, assuming the requisite permission (which may well need to come from a foreign government) to be forthcoming. As to this, where the proposed investigation is sponsored by a learned and respected institution and has the financial support of influential organizations, a favourable response may usually be anticipated. The leader of a more modest expedition, on the other hand, may well find it necessary to conduct his negotiations at a less elevated level, where the probability is that he will encounter members of an indifferent officialdom, with all its attendant frustrations.

In an instructive account of how, in the course of three years spent in Turkish territory, he and his associates wasted more time arguing with customs men (not to mention coast guards, army representatives, naval officers, and various categories of police—local, revenue, military, and secret) than was devoted to diving or, indeed, to any other useful activity, Peter Throckmorton[136] goes on to explain:

> My trouble was that I believed that all these difficulties could be solved reasonably. If my equipment was stuck in customs, there must be a correct way to get it out. I could not understand that the customs man had no intention of ever letting it out. Our application for permission to use the equipment had been submitted to higher authorities, who would in turn submit it to yet higher authorities, until someday, along with thousands of others,

our petition would arrive on the desk of the person who would make the decision. When would it arrive? A year from now, two years, who knew? Why bother? The answer would inevitably be 'Yok' (No).

The mission, nevertheless, proved unexpectedly worthwhile. Much of Throckmorton's heel-kicking was done in Bodrum (ancient Halicarnassus) where, in the course of conversations with resident fishermen and sponge divers, he learned of the existence of large accumulations of amphorae at a place called Yassi Ada (Flat Island), and of a heap of copper ingots to be found in the vicinity of Cape Gelidonya. And after satisfying himself as to the genuineness of these accounts, he returned to America, where he eventually succeeded in gaining the interest of Dr. Rodney Young, of the University of Pennsylvania Museum, who introduced him to his assistant, George F. Bass. Within a week, the decision to investigate the sites had been taken, subject to the availability of the necessary finance. . . .

Governmental assistance, it would seem, is usually reserved for projects considered to involve national interest or prestige, as in the case of the Antikythera wreck and, more recently, that of the *Vasa*. Fortunately, experience also tends to show that, at any rate in academic circles, fund raising for an approved archaeological undertaking seldom presents any insuperable obstacles, and in the present instance the Pennsylvania Museum advanced the equivalent of some £4,000 towards the cost of the proposed Anatolian venture, other useful contributions coming from the Rockefeller Foundation, the National Geographic Society, and kindred organizations, as well as from private citizens. Thanks to these donations, a sum large enough to finance a comparable land excavation was collected. This sufficed to cover the cost of the undertaking, notwithstanding the pessimistic prediction earlier made by James Dugan[48] about the relative outgoings of a wet and a dry dig—he had expressed the view that the amount of money needed for the one would be ten times that required for the other, having regard for the necessity of providing a research ship and ancilliary vessels, fully manned, and to employ well paid experts (as opposed to the unskilled labour so freely available on land) including teams of divers whose effective working period would be severely curtailed by decompression schedules and other underwater disciplines, not to mention inclement weather.

It may be accepted that the most expensive single (and exclusively marine) item is likely to be the research ship, which, ideally, needs to be a sea-going vessel sufficiently large to carry a great deal of heavy equipment (including auxilliary engines and air compressors) in addition to providing living accommodation for the crew and a score or more members of the expedition. But the outright purchase of a workboat specially designed and built for archaeological purposes must remain a dream realizable only by the few,* though even among those of modest means, private ambitions to acquire and operate a ship of their own have nevertheless shown themselves to be within the bounds of accomplishment, as the efforts of J. Y. Cousteau[33] and his early G.E.R.S. associates (Tailliez and Dumas) go to show. For although the *Élie Monnier* sufficed well enough for a time, the three men were all the while discussing and planning the building of a craft to their own design. When approached about the idea, however, the naval authorities were not disposed to offer much encouragement ('Work for advancement until you are an admiral! Then you might get your ship!' Cousteau, a lowly lieutenant-commander, was informed).

It was shortly after being given this gratuitous advice that the recipient remembered an earlier meeting with an acquaintance of some affluence who had expressed an interest in underwater activities. The upshot was a visit to the dockyards of Malta, and the acquisition of a 140-feet long ex-Royal Navy minesweeper, built in the U.S.A. in 1942. The vessel was delivered to Antibes for a refit, in the course of which it underwent extensive alterations, including the provision of a diving well amidships, a high observation bridge, and an underwater viewing chamber, located externally of the bow structure, at

---

*Of whom Edwin A. Link is one, thanks to the commercial success of the well known aviation trainer which bears his name. In 1951 he became interested in the supposed remains of an ancient galleon (which on investigation proved to be those of an 18th century British frigate!) and he was thus led to buy and convert his first boat, *Sea Diver*. This sufficed until, after roaming the Caribbean for several years in search of Spanish gold, in 1956 he designed and ordered the construction of *Sea Diver II*, 100-feet long and with a cruising range of 7,000 miles. It was in this magnificent craft, replete with every conceivable kind of diving aid that, after investigating the remains of Port Royal (see below), Link made his way to the Mediterranean, where he carried out investigations among the islands of the Aegean and elsewhere.

the end of which it emerged as the undersea research ship *Calypso*.

Even in the absence of a wealthy sponsor, however, boats and other essential equipment can be borrowed or hired for the occasion, while other costs can be kept down by resorting to various expedients. Thus the help of volunteer divers can readily be enlisted, not necessarily to the detriment of the outcome of the undertaking. Advantage, at all events, can always be taken

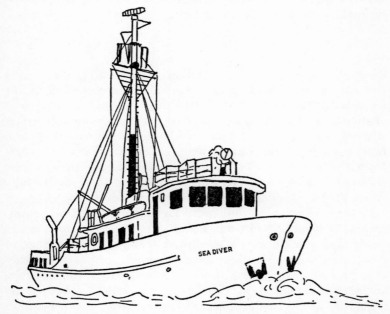

31. Edwin A. Link's underwater research ship Sea Diver *(based on a photograph).*

of the services offered by the *Confédération Mondiale des Activités Subacquatiques,* an international organization which maintains a register of competent divers, both amateur and professional, who are familiar with the conditions which exist in various parts of the world's seas.

This all-important question of personnel, and of their relationship with, and the extent of the control exercised by, the leader of an underwater mission is touched upon by Frédéric

Dumas,[50] who takes as his example a sizable ancient wreck located at a depth of 100 feet or so. In the light of his long and varied experience (more than 2,500 descents in the first decade of the aqualung), he advocates the use of a boat of up to 300 tons (*Calypso*=360 tons), manned by a work team which includes a professional diver accompanied by as many as a dozen assistants (half of whom may be amateurs), plus at least four draughtsmen and two photographers. Significantly (doubly so, since he himself is a diver), his list of underwater operators is headed by the words *an archaeologist*.

IV

Once the need for the active intervention of archaeologists in the excavation of underwater sites had been conceded by the community of divers, and no less reluctantly acknowledged in academic circles, the question of representation at once arose, whereupon it became apparent that any such participation must come from the younger members of the profession. Apart from any want of enthusiasm for the task displayed by senior colleagues, not only were these gentlemen likely to be fully committed to other duties and interests, but the probability was that they would be found sadly lacking in one vital qualification: outstanding physical fitness.

Medical practitioners have listed a depressing number of disabilities which should exclude a man (or woman) from engaging in deep diving. These ailments range from obesity and defective vision to diseases of the lungs, intestinal irregularities, and cardiovascular abnormalities, not to mention any tendency towards emotional immaturity, personality disorders, or neurotic trends. Sufferers from asthma, hay fever, mastoiditis, migraine, and claustrophobia are likewise specifically barred, as are alcoholics and drug addicts (including excessive smokers of tobacco), together with the luckless possessors of hemorrhoids, varicose veins, and a doubtful genitourinary condition. As a precautionary measure, an annual fitness test is earnestly recommended, and the marvel is, perhaps, that any candidates at all succeed in passing it. And in order to do so, it would appear that the prime requisite is youthfulness—not over the age of 30 insofar as Service recruits

28. Diving barge anchored above Byzantine and Roman wrecks at Yassi Ada. **29.** Plotting the position of amphorae marking the Byzantine wreck. (Photos: *George F. Bass*)

30. Partly excavated hull of the Roman vessel, here shown *in situ* at a depth of 140 feet. The white markers indicate the position of wooden dowels (treenails) used in the hull construction. **31.** The two-man submarine *Asherah*, used at Yassi Ada and elsewhere to locate and study the wrecks of ships. (Photos: *George F. Bass*)

are concerned, if the recommendations of R. H. Davis[41] be accepted.

On the other hand, merely learning how to operate the aqualung offers no problem—Honor Frost[60] has recorded the initiation of a beginner aged 75, while under the expert tuition of Frédélic Dumas, trainee divers of the G.E.R.S., destined for a career in the French Navy, were taught to make descents of 130 feet in a matter of days. In recent years, similar establishments have been opened in a number of countries, including Great Britain,* where learners can undergo a preliminary course of training. And in the process, the prospective leader of an underwater archaeological expedition will need to familiarize himself with a multitude of tasks, for the efficient carrying out of which the ultimate responsibility will be his.

Among other duties, he will need to ensure that all diving equipment is regularly serviced and maintained in good working order—e.g., that compressed air cylinders are not left lying about in the hot sun, or charged above their rated figure, or inadvertently filled with other than breathable air;† he must keep a constant check on the state of the weather, observe the temperature of the water, plan the day's operations, and see to it that no man is permitted to dive if he is tired, or is suffering from a cold in the head, or is in any way indisposed; and once the members of a team of divers have made their descent, the duration of their stay underwater must on no account be allowed to exceed permissible depth-time limits, while in the event of an emergency, there must be an ability instantly to recognize the various forms of decompression sickness, coupled with a knowledge of the whereabouts of the nearest available recompression chamber.

*A Committee for Nautical Archaeology was formed in 1964, composed of representatives from such institutions as the British Museum, the Science Museum, the National Maritime Museum, the Society for Nautical Research, the National Institute of Oceanography, and the Institute of Archaeology, where its headquarters are based. In 1969, the Committee established a School for Nautical Archaeology at Plymouth (S.N.A.P.), in association with Plymouth Ocean Projects (P.O.P.). In charge are Jim Gill, Owen Gander, and (Lieutenant-Commander) Alan Bax, and the School is housed in Fort Bovisand, replete with a small harbour, leased from the Ministry of Defence.

†In 1946 the three leaders of the G.E.R.S. had a lucky escape when the contents of their air cyclinders were found to be mixed with carbon-monoxide gas, as a result of the compressor intake valve being located close to the exhaust of an internal combustion engine; experience has also shown that the flashing of lubrication oil in the air compressor cylinder is also a possible source of contamination

The underwater aspirant will also need to learn how to acquire a sense of position in the absence of a horizon, and in a medium in which he is suspended in hydrostatic balance and able to move about freely in three dimensions. Normally, in clear water, the lighter region above him can be relied upon to indicate the position of the surface, though this is not necessarily an infallible guide. At the half-way mark where the total depth, say, is 160 feet, reflected light from the unseen sea-bed will match the intensity of that coming from overhead, with the result that a diver's state of disorientation may be such that he is unable to distinguish between up and down. His response in such an extremity must be to cease all conscious movement, watch the direction taken by the bubbles emerging from his breathing apparatus, and then follow them to the surface. If the water is so lacking in clarity that the bubbles are difficult to discern, and his air supply is nearly depleted, his plight may well be serious, as there can be no question of his using his other sensory processes. Those relating to touch, taste, and smell are clearly inapplicable, nor can reliance be placed upon audition, as in subaqueous surroundings it is virtually impossible to determine whence a sound comes. This is because the direction finding ability of the human ear depends upon the slight difference in time at which the signals arrive at each separate organ of hearing, a disparity in response to which the head adjusts to the situation by turning towards the source. But it so happens that the speed of sound in water is between four and five times faster than it is in air, in consequence of which the time delay is so reduced that, in the absence of an electronic aid, any attempted interpretation of direction is frustrated.

Finding one's way under water (apart from the fact that the sense of touch can be invoked when following a guide line) is thus largely dependent upon visual sensation, and the process may either be one of pilotage (entailing a noting of recognizable topographical features) or of navigation, assisted by the use of such instruments as a compass, a depth gauge, and a watch. The last-named may usefully be fitted with a dial which merely registers the passing of minutes, since it is not the hour of the day that matters, but the total time that has elapsed since the start of a dive. A watch may also serve to determine the extent of a journey when the rate of travel in a given direction is known (speed × time = distance).

All this, and more, forms an indispensable part of the curriculum of the student diver, and provides a necessary addition to the knowledge that any intending underwater archaeologist will already possess concerning the examination and excavation of a site—except that established methods relate almost exclusively to a dry environment. New techniques are thus called for, about which there is much to be learned from efforts made in recent years, in terms of what, and what not, should be done. As to this, although in the past many mistakes were undoubtedly made, useful skills were nevertheless developed and a considerable understanding gained, and if this valuable experience is not to be wasted, there is clearly a need for close and continuing collaboration between divers and archaeologists, that a standard code of underwater procedure may be evolved and applied.

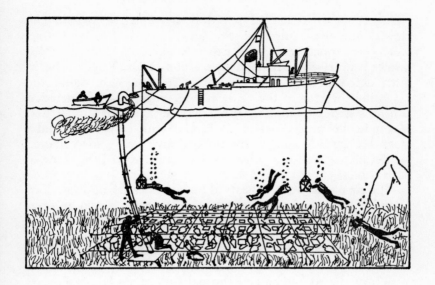

Chapter Seven

The Way Ahead

I

Investigators in Italy were provided with an opportunity of examining another newly found wreck when Gianni Roghi became interested in the remains of (what proved to be) a Roman ship dating from 120–100 B.C. The vessel had been discovered, in about 60 feet of water, situated between the northern coast of Sardinia and the island of Spargi, in the vicinity of a *secca* which rose abruptly from the sea-bed to within a short distance of the surface—the evident cause of the disaster.

The excavation was planned to start early in 1958. It was to be undertaken, moreover, with the avowed intention of making a detailed and painstaking survey, involving a stratigraphical approach which would entail lifting the entire cargo and recovering anything that remained of the ship itself. And although this ambitious programme was not destined to be carried out in its entirety, it duly began as arranged. The underwater team consisted of a cameraman and nine amateur divers, equipped with large capacity aqualungs, all of whom worked under the personal supervision of Dr. Roghi, who in turn acted in collaboration with Professor Lamboglia, the scientific director of the undertaking. Support craft included a fishing smack (complete with a derrick), a motor launch, and a couple of rowing boats, in addition to which a pontoon and a deep-sea tug belonging to the Italian Navy were also available, while the research ship *Diano* in due course visited the scene of operations.

The first task was to locate the site, mark its position, and then lay floats and mooring buoys. The wreck lay on an even keel under a cover of sand from which there sprouted a forest of poseidon weed. Attempts to clear this tenacious growth, first with a rake, and then by means of a sickle, were ineffective, until use was made of a three-pronged tool which could penetrate the ground and cut through the accumulation of roots.

Once the site had been cleared it was found that, apart from those jars which projected from the surface of the burial mound, the ship's cargo of amphorae seemingly remained in the position in which it had been stored, neatly stacked layer upon layer in a manner which promised greatly to assist their surveyal. This was a task which involved the use of two grids made of yellow canvas tape, composed of 2-metre squares, individually identifiable by lettering which ran from A to Q, and from AA to QQ. Each grid, wound round a pole and handled by three men in a boat, was conveyed to its underwater location in the following manner: a pair of divers, swimming backwards from the boat, unrolled the tape network until it lay spread out upon the surface of the sea. They were then joined by two colleagues, who assisted in taking the grid down to the sea-bed, where it was stretched over the site and held in place, at the required height, by attaching it to wooden posts. As these stakes displayed a tendency to float free, it was found necessary to drive them into position to a depth of two feet or so.

The grid squares were then systematically photographed from a predetermined height. All told, some 500 pictures were taken (in colour as well as in black and white), the cameraman hovering above the amphora field, endeavouring all the while to maintain his position despite the presence of a considerable undertow—a most exhausting experience. From the information thus obtained, a photo mosaic was prepared, upon which each visible amphora was assigned its own number. Small plaques were then used to apply this figuring to the items of the cargo, a task which was accomplished, a square at a time, with the aid of photographic enlargements, marked in indelible ink for underwater use. Later in the preceedings, these prints were replaced by a blackboard equivalent, upon which the necessary details had previously been sketched in chalk, though both systems gave rise to problems of identification, either because some of the photographs were lacking in clarity,* or because there was a want of accuracy on the part of the artist. In view of these difficulties, the procedure was eventually reversed, the diver first numbering the jars, and then marking his board. It was ultimately concluded (and accepted) that, particularly where the topmost layers of a cargo of stacked amphorae are concerned, exact numbering was unlikely to be achieved, as some confusion was unavoidably caused by jars which occupied an intermediate position.

With the completion of the initial phase of the numbering, the first of the two grids was removed and the lifting of the cargo begun. A novel feature of the air-lift used in the excavation was that it was of plastic construction, and consisted of flanged segments of pipe with joints of rubberized canvas, thus combining lightness (which made for ease of handling) with flexibility. Various methods of discharge were tried—on board ship, by way of a length of armoured hose directly into a sieve, and at surface level, without screening—though at the intake end, an experimental removal of the filter nozzle, in an effort to improve suction, had to be abandoned: it led to a constant

---

*Occasioned in part by the turbidity of the water, brought about by the outpourings of a torrent on the Sardinian coast. During the photographing of the squares, it also became evident that these had been made too large. To line them up in his viewfinder, the cameraman needed to station himself at a height of thirteen feet, with consequent loss of picture detail. As a result of this experience, grid squares not exceeding the metric equivalent of five feet by five feet have since been advocated, so as to allow a maximum operational height of ten feet above the field. As for sites whose immediate surroundings are excessively muddy, this is a situation which can be countered by making use of a truncated cone of transparent material which is filled with clear water, either at the surface (Dumas[50]) or when submerged (Bass[9]), and placed over the object to be photographed.

blockage of the pipe and to the wasting of much time in clearing it.

The amphorae were raised in the customary wire basket, and at the end of a month (which brought the first season's work to a close) the second grid had been removed and the remainder of the topmost layer of the cargo brought to the surface. A count revealed that, in all, some 300 jars had been raised, of which about one third were intact. They were of two main types which, with few exceptions, bore Greek markings, and their removal from the site enabled the outline of the ship to be more clearly distinguished. It at all events became possible to make out what appeared to be the bow of the vessel, and to estimate that its overall dimensions weer about 99 feet long by 27 feet wide. Its total cargo of jars was put at about 3,000, a normal load for a freight-carrier of the Republican Period.

Thus far, in addition to amphorae, there had been retrieved such predictable items as pottery and portions of lead sheathing from the hull. But when work was resumed in the following year, there took place the first recorded instance of the finding of a part of the skeleton of an ancient Greek or Roman seaman, in the guise of a human skull, wearing the still recognizable remnants of what had once been a helmet! Other events associated with the second season's work, however, were of a less gratifying nature. As the lifting of the cargo continued, it gave rise to ever increasing confusion, the purposeful removal of one amphorae leading to an involuntary displacement of others, prior to which the return to the site had been greeted by another and no less unwelcome discovery. An examination of the bow section, in the vicinity of which parts of the ship's woodwork had earlier been found, revealed that of this, next to nothing now remained. The fragile timbers, left exposed and unprotected, had disintegrated and vanished, thus bringing forcibly to notice one more environmental lesson that needed to be learned.

II

In reporting on what had been accomplished thus far (and prior to the untimely demise of Dr. Roghi), Nino Lamboglia, in affirming that some progress had been achieved in the realm of underwater excavation and recording, added that the next step must be in the direction of the more difficult task of making sections—a problem which, as it happened, had recently been tackled by a team of French divers, under the combined leadership of Frédéric Dumas (representing the G.E.R.S.) and Alex Sirvirine (of the O.F.R.S.). This activity concerned what came to be distinguished as the Dramont A wreck, so-called after the Cape of that name near St. Raphael, where a submarine ridge, a mere three feet or so from the surface of the water, extends seawards from a small island, itself a prolongation of the Cape. Here, in 1956, at some distance from the foot of the ridge, Claude Santamaria unexpectedly came upon the remains of an amphora carrier. Apparently, the combined action of strong currents and a sloping terrain had caused the stricken vessel to slide a distance of 90 yards beyond the reef before it came to rest in 100 feet of water, a circumstance which helped to explain why it had not been noticed earlier.

A cursory examination of the site was made by Santamaria and his fellow members of the local diving club, who reached the conclusion that it gave promise of being of particular archaeological interest, if only because of the multiplicity of marks displayed by the small number of storage jars they managed to bring up. In the year following its discovery, however, plunderers attacked the wreck with explosives, causing havoc to the upper layers of its cargo, whereupon Fernand Benoit called for the making of a more detailed investigation before it was too late, in response to which the joint G.E.R.S. and O.F.R.S. expedition arrived on the scene in August, 1959. Their support vessel was the *Espadon*, a substantial fishing boat which had been acquired for use as an auxilliary on occasions when the *Calypso* was otherwise engaged.

With the limited time at their disposal, anything approaching a complete excavation was out of the question, and the investigators decided to dig an exploratory trench across the wreck amidships, by which means it was hoped to obtain both a representative sample of the vessel's cargo and a section of its hull. The first task was to remove extraneous amphorae, in the course of which broken pieces (of which there proved to be many) were piled up outside the limits of the site, while any

whole specimens were raised to the surface. Trenching then
began, accompanied by photographing and charting, and aided
by the outsize air-lift which had been used at Grand Congloué.
The hose, with its diameter of more than four and a half inches,
was so heavy that it needed to be supported at its upper end, and
in the rough seas about Cape Dramont, wave action was
transmitted down the length of the pipe to such an extent as to
render its lower extremity uncontrollable. This problem had
earlier been encountered by members of the *Club d'Etude
Sous-Marines* of Tunis during their work on the Mahdia wreck,
and their answer had been to suspend the pipe from a submerged float anchored to the sea-bed, so that the discharge
took place under water, i.e., in a relatively calm region. A
similar solution was adopted at Cape Dramont, though no
attempt was made to filter the tube's outpourings, so that,
while mud and sand were carried away by the current, sherds
and other items fell back onto the site. This, however, constituted more of an annoyance than a danger, though it may be
noted in passing that when the Pennsylvania University team
experienced this trouble at Yassi Ada (*vide post*), its members
abated the nuisance by capping the pipe outlet with a wire
cage and a cloth bag, a combination which entrapped sea
shells and the like, and yet did not impede the escape of sand
and mud particles.

As the excavation of the Dramont wreck progressed, it
became apparent that the entire cargo was much damaged and
in a state of the utmost confusion, though a tendency for it to
lean in a particular direction was noticed, and attributed to
the shock of impact. The first part of the hull to be encountered
was so insubstantial that it disintegrated in front of the air-lift.
Thereafter, care was taken to remove sand from timber by
fanning it into a cloud of suspended matter which could then
be swept up from a safe distance. The woodwork thus revealed
had become so soft and yielding as a result of its long immersion
that the heavy cargo was found to have broken through it and
spilled between the closely spaced ribs. Eventually, however,
an area of double skin planking was uncovered, and this was
sawn across and removed, to provide a glimpse of a worm-
ridden keel complete with garboards, a section of which was
likewise recovered. Subsequent examination (by Fernand

Benoit) suggested that in addition to a keel, the bottom of the ship contained a keelson, whose associated rib structure seemingly alternated between half timbers (as at Grand Congloué) and whole timbers (as at Titan), thus affording evidence of the use of an intermediate form of construction.

Among additional objects recovered were examples of kitchen pottery, a fragment of a helmet, and a much corroded *aes*, which coin, however, was so badly disfigured that its date could not be determined. But the main interest centred on the amphorae which had been brought up, thanks to the profusion of marks they displayed—Bac (Bacchius), Dam (Dama), Evta (Evtaclus), Onel (Onellus), Pilip (Pilipus), Herm (Hermaores) —several of which, e.g., Heraclid (Heraclides) had not previously been encountered.

III

Up to the start of the 1960s, American participation in underwater events in the Mediterranean had been restricted to the activities of a few individuals, notable amongst whom, apart from the legendary Guy Gilpatrick, was James Dugan, whose close and continuing association with J. Y. Cousteau and the *Calypso* expeditions began at the end of World War II. Yet a third, if somewhat more recent member of the small band of New World expatriates was Peter Throckmorton, at once an erstwhile student of anthropology, an occasional diver, and the possessor of a wanderlust which eventually brought him to Turkey by way of Hawaii, France, and Afghanistan.

In 1958, at the Carian port of Bodrum, centre of the Turkish sponge industry, he learned of the existence of a cargo of Bronze Age copper ingots, strewn about the sea-bed in the neighbourhood of Cape Gelidonya, a desolate coastal region some 185 miles to the south. His informant was a Captain Kemal Aras, who had happened upon the site some years previously. After visiting the place and satisfying himself of the worth of the story, Throckmorton, as earlier recounted, returned to America, where he succeeded in gaining the interest of the University of Pennsylvania Museum, at that time already engaged in land excavations in Annatolia.

George F. Bass, then a research assistant at the Museum, was appointed director of the undertaking, with Throckmorton as assistant director and photographer. Honor Frost, who had met and worked with Throckmorton at Bodrum, was assigned the post of architect and draughtsman, while the services of Frédéric Dumas were also obtained: he was enlisted as chief diver. Apart from the director, all the leading members of the team were seasoned underwater swimmers, a circumstance which placed George Bass at a disadvantage which he promptly sought to overcome by taking a crash course in diving— experience would (and did) come later. Among other indispensable members of the expedition were Joan du Plat Taylor, whose staff duties concerned the dating and preservation of finds, and Kemal Aras, the discoverer of the site, who served as guide and was placed in charge of the boats—the *Mandalinci* and the *Lufti Gelil*, both fishing craft from Bodrum, hired for the occasion. A dinghy equipped with an outboard motor was also available.

The scene of the wreck was a row of half a dozen offshore islets, around which strong currents endlessly surged over jagged rocks, some of which were barely awash. The adjacent mainland was as wild as it was inhospitable, devoid of roads and approachable only from the sea, and as the neighbourhood of the islands offered no facilities for establishing camp, these had to be sought elsewhere. Two prime considerations were a supply of fresh water and a safe anchorage for the boats, both of which were eventually found, an hour's sailing distance away, in the shape of a small cove with a secluded beach. Here, living quarters were set up, complete with work rooms and a machine repair shop.

Examination of the wreck showed that what remained of the ship's contents occupied a compact area, covered by a depth of water which varied between 90 and 95 feet. Little in the way of material evidence was immediately to be seen, as the vessel had settled on rock but thinly covered with sand, and most of its woodwork had long since vanished. Vestiges of planking, however, were later found in places where some protection had been afforded by overlying cargo, which in turn had become heavily encrusted with a calcareous deposit.

As a first move, the area was surveyed and mapped. Triangulately measurements were taken from spikes driven into the ground, which information was recorded underwater on translucent plastic sheets, thus establishing the relative positions of scattered groups of objects. The accuracy of this overall plan was then checked against an overhead photographic view, prepared by a diver who swam at a predetermined height above the sea-bed with the assistance of a level and a plumb-line attachment to his camera. The use of standard measuring rods to mark the site enabled a series of uniform prints to be made which, by judicious editing, were then joined to provide a true-to-scale composite picture.

As the main wreck area was limited, the expedition's eight divers worked two or three at a time, each team member descending twice a day and spending 40 minutes underwater in the course of the morning, and 28 minutes during the afternoon, after allowing for a period of at least 3 hours between one descent and the next. As an additional precaution, each return from the depths called for the making of a decompression stop of 6 minutes at a distance of 10 feet below the surface, while a line, fastened to a rock within the excavation area, indicated the shortest route to the diving boat in the event of an emergency.

For clearing the outskirts of the site, some use was made of two air-lifts, but much of the sand covering the wreck itself was moved by hand, and conveyed to the surface in buckets for sifting. A metal detector was also employed, and this instrument revealed the presence of scattered items which might otherwise have been missed. The bulk of the cargo, however, was in the form of large lumps of conjoined metal, thick with a hard concretion by which it was firmly cemented to the sea-floor. In order to save time and to avoid the possibility of damaging individual artifacts by attempting to extract them where they lay, it was decided to raise these solidified heaps *en masse*, once they had been freed by cutting them loose with hammer and chisel. On occasion, this activity produced two or more large pieces, which were afterwards put together, that their contents might be considered as a single entity during the process of dismemberment and examination. Meanwhile, though much of this material was winched to the surface at the end of a cables, those pieces which were found to have remnants of the ship's timbers adhering to them required more careful handling. This

32. Balloon lift at Cape Gelidonya (as depicted in an original painting by Davis Meltzer).

was achieved by means of an innovation which Frédéric Dumas introduced, in the shape of a plastic balloon which was attached to the object to be lifted, inflated from an air-hose, and then sent on its way aloft.

From the nature and disposition of the cargo, the wreck was adjudged to have been a small sailing ship, some 35 feet long, which sank while engaged in transporting a load of copper from the mines of Cyprus, though both the nationality of the vessel and its intended destination remained a matter of conjecture. Interestingly enough, the metal cargo, which weighed over a ton, was found to consist of finished products as well as raw material. Much of this last was in the guise of four-handled copper ingots, bearing signs which were identified as belonging to the as yet undeciphered Cypro-Minoan script. But in addition to ingots cast in the familiar 'ox-hide' shape, there were others in the form of slabs and discs. Nor was this all, for in places the metal was found to have protected and preserved mounds of white powder, which on analysis proved to be stannic oxide. Moreover, in addition to the essential constituents of bronze—copper and tin—the cargo also consisted of many implements which had been fashioned out of this alloy. The majority of these items had evidently served an agricultural purpose, in that they consisted of picks, hoes, axes, and shovels. Most of them, however, were broken, and as they were found in association with ingot fragments, it was concluded that in addition to its load of ingredients for making bronze, the ship also carried scrap alloy for melting down.

A balance pan, complete with several sets of weights, was also recovered. In one of these sets, the smallest unit matched the ancient Egyptian *qedet*, a standard known to have been used both in Cyprus and Syria. Sundry pieces of pottery which could have emanated from these or neighbouring regions, were of added importance because they gave an indication of date— Joan du Plat Taylor considered them to be of thirteenth century origin, probably within a few years of 1200 B.C., an estimation subsequently confirmed by radio carbon measurements.

Prior to 1947, archaeological methods of age determination were often restricted to the making of a typological or a stratigraphical approach, which merely provided relative, as opposed to absolute, dates. Thus an indication of the age of an artifact could be obtained by comparing it with an identical object from another source, something of the history of which was already known. Alternatively, during the examination of an undisturbed and stratified site, it could be safely assumed that items found in a lower level were earlier than those contained in an upper level.* But what such sequence dating could not by itself reveal was the age of the various finds in terms of years, and the importance of the radio carbon method of dating is that it is able to provide this information.

*While it will be evident that this is a circumstance which does not apply to a shipwreck and its contents, which collectively represent a closed deposit, i.e., an assemblage of objects which were in use at one time at a fixed date, the order of loading of a mixed cargo can clearly be of importance in determining ports of call and probable destination.

The technique is based in the discovery (details of which were published by W. F. Libby, E. C. Anderson, and others in 1947) of the presence in the atmosphere of an unstable isotope (atomic variant) of carbon of mass 14. Together with ordinary carbon (mass 12), the $C14$, in the form of gaseous carbon dioxide, is absorbed by plants and so finds its way into animal tissues, as earlier noted. As a result, all living things are rendered faintly radioactive by virtue of assimilated $C14$, the rate of distintegration of which is such that it loses half its substance every 5,600 years. Otherwise expressed, in that length of time, 32 pounds of the isotope will have been reduced to 16 pounds, and at the end of another such period, the 16 pounds will have become 8 pounds, and so on. Furthermore, during the lifetime

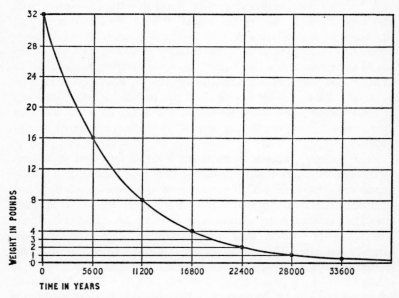

33. *Atomic disintegration of Carbon 14. The fraction of the total number of atoms in a given quantity of a radio-active substance which breaks down in unit time is constant, i.e., the activity diminishes exponentially with time. The period after which half the atoms have disintegrated is termed the half-life period, which for C-14 amounts to some 5,600 years. At the end of this period, 32 pounds of the material will have become 32/2 = 16 pounds, and after another such interval, the 16 pounds will have been reduced to 16/2 = 8 pounds, and so on.*

32. The underwater telephone booth, as installed at Yassi Ada.
(Photo: *George F. Bass*)

33. Ship outline, carved on the rock face of the approach to the Acropolis at Lindos, Island of Rhodes. **34.** Relics of lost Atlantis? Storage jars at the Palace of Minos, Knossos, Crete. (Photos: *the Author*)

of a recipient, a balance establishes itself between the amount of $C14$ that is absorbed, and the amount that is lost through radioactive decay. But with the death of a plant or an animal, assimilation ceases, and the process of disintegration is left to go on alone. In effect, the emitted radiation grows progressively weaker with the passing of time, and by measuring the strength of these signals (by Geiger counter or other means), the number of years that have elapsed since, say, a tree was felled to become part of a boat, can be calculated, plus or minus a small margin of experimental error. The process, which is applicable to any form of organic carbon, e.g., that contained in the bones of animals, is accurate over a minimum period of 50,000 years.

Although the largest piece of the ship's hull raised at Cape Gelidonya measured no more than 3 feet across, other arboreal material which was recovered aroused considerable speculation as to its intended purpose. It consisted of a large bundle of well preserved tree branches, with bark and twigs still on them, and from the position in which these sticks were found, Bass[9] has since come to the significant conclusion that they were intended to serve as dunnage. For this finding, in turn, throws new light on a hitherto obscure passage in Homer,[76] describing how Odysseus, with the reluctant assistance of the goddess Calypso, built himself a boat with which to make his escape from his island prison. In the past, translators of the original Greek wording have described the provision of osier twigs as constituting a form of wattle fence designed to afford 'some protection against the heavy seas'. The relevant passage, Bass now suggests, should be given the more literal rendering that Odysseus merely 'heaped up a great deal of brushwood', intended to serve as an inner lining.

IV

Although the leaders of the University of Pennsylvania's first underwater archaeological expedition had good reason to be fully satisfied with the outcome of their activities,* the fact

*In the course of which, claims Bass (in company with Joan du Plat Taylor[134]), archaeologists and divers were for the first time brought together on the sea-bed, in what Frédéric Dumas afterwards described as 'the first methodical excavation carried to completion'.

remained that Cape Gelidonya was not typical of the majority
of known Mediterranean sites, in that the sandy conditions
necessary to ensure the preservation of a substantial portion of
the ship's hull were lacking. But while it was not possible for the
investigators to provide a graphic reconstruction of the vessel,
such as that relating to the Albenga wreck which Nino
Lamboglia was soon to publish (*Rivista di Studi Liguri*, XXVII,
Bordighera, 1961), the excavation was nevertheless deemed to
be of historical interest, if only because it had resulted in the
recovery of a cargo of metal which proved to be 'by far the
largest hoard of pre-Classical copper and bronze implements
ever found in the Aegean area'.

Next to receive attention was the much more extensive
wreck site which Peter Throckmorton had discovered at Yassi
Ada. This island was the last of a group of eight, to the west of
which there lurked a barely submerged reef, invisible to approaching mariners—'a very subtle ship trap'. Even a cursory
examination of the vicinity satisfied Throckmorton that down
through the years, it had become the graveyard of a score or
more ships. He and Honor Frost collected a number of jars,
drawings of which were submitted to an acknowledged authority
(in the person of Virginia Grace, of the American School of
Archaeology in Athens) for identification and dating. On
typological grounds, one of the wrecks was assigned to the first
century A.D., while others, which lay in deeper water, appeared
to be Late Roman, ranging from the fourth to seventh centuries
A.D.

The wreck selected by Bass and his team lay at a depth of
120 feet, and to assist in carrying out the work, additional
staff were recruited and assembled at Bodrum, where workshops
were established. At Yassi Ada, some 16 miles distant, field
headquarters were set up on a large barge, anchored a hundred
yards from its shores—the island itself was overrun with rats.
However, after members of the resident population had
demonstrated an ability to swim out to the barge, camp was
later made in their midst, in specially screened areas.

After the wreck had been cleaned of seaweed, all visible
objects were labelled and numbered, and the task of plotting
their positions begun. Dumas had earlier devised a tubular
frame, complete with calibrated sliding members, which was

intended to be placed over the site, thereby enabling co-ordinates and levels quickly to be noted by a single diver. In practice, however, it was found that time was wasted rather than saved by the contrivance, and it was soon replaced by a less ambitious system of wire squares. After recordings had been made by artists, who sketched on gridded plastic sheets, the lifting of the uppermost layer of the cargo was begun, an operation which yielded about 100 globular type amphorae, the first of an estimated 900 such items. Sand covering the second layer of jars was then removed with an air-lift, and the process repeated.

By the end of the third season's work, in addition to many amphorae, the area of the wreck had yielded 11 anchors, a large collection of pottery, and 48 coins, two-thirds of which were copper, the remainder gold. The head which appeared most often on this metallic currency was that of the Byzantine Emperor Heraclius I (reigned A.D. 610–641), enabling the wreck to be dated with exactitude, and placing in it the first half of the seventh century. Nor was this the only identification that was made. On a steelyard, inscribed in Greek, were the proprietorial words: George Senior Sea Captain. Even the forms of no longer existing artifacts were recovered, thanks to the restorative expertise developed by Michael Katzev. He specialized in the sectioning of pieces of concretion gathered from the site, an activity undertaken in the knowledge that as iron rusts away on the sea-bed, it acquires a hard protective coating of sand and lime, wherein an impression of the original object is to be found. By cutting the concretions with an electric saw, the two halves of a mould were produced, thus making it possible to reproduce a wide variety of shapes with the aid of a synthetic rubber casting material. Items reconstituted in this manner included a shovel, a hoe, a set of bill hooks, an adze, chisels, pick axes, files, and a sack of nails.

The ship's woodwork, meanwhile, had likewise required expert attention. When the vessel's timbers were first un-covered, they displayed a tendency to come adrift and float away—the iron nails used to fasten the planking had long since vanished. This difficulty was overcome by pinning the remains of the wreck with hundreds of cycle wheel spokes, an impro-visation which sufficed to hold the timberwork together until

34. *Method of recovering lengths of fragile timber, as introduced during underwater operations at Yassi Ada (after Davis Meltzer).*

it was fully exposed and could be examined and photographed, prior to its being dismantled and brought to the surface. This last operation called for the utmost care in handling, and it was accomplished with the aid of a custom-built wire basket, some 18 feet long. The fragile lengths of timber were placed in this container, and then carried to the island by divers who walked with it across and up the slope of the intervening sea-bed.

The demanding task of reconstructing the wreck on paper was entrusted to Frederick van Doornick, a graduate student of archaeology and the expedition's second in command. After four seasons spent in mapping and recording every stage of the excavation, van Doornick then devoted another three years to assembling the evidence thus made available. Thanks to a meticulous and painstaking attention to detail, in the course of which (in the words of George Bass) he studied the position of every tiny artifact and fragment of rotted wood, and pondered the meaning of every notch and nail hole, the result of his efforts surpassed all expectations.

The picture of the ship which emerged was more or less complete from keel to deck beams, and provided an accurate portrayal, apart from certain assumptions made in respect of hull curvature. It depicted a vessel between 60 and 70 feet long, and some 17 feet wide, and it was apparent that while the main part of the hull had been constructed in the time-honoured fashion (planks laid on edge to form a shell, into which ribs were afterwards inserted), this did not apply to an upper section, where the procedure had been reversed. Here, boards had been fastened to an existing framework, in the modern manner, thus indicating, it may be, that by the seventh century A.D., ship-building in the Mediterranean was in a state of transition.

Subsequent activities in the vicinity of the Byzantine site involved the excavation of a number of other wrecks,* assisted by the introduction of new and improved devices which ranged from a track-mounted air-lift and a towed observation capsule to a two-man submarine (the *Asherah*), fitted with a pair of aerial survey cameras. Consideration was also given to the problem of communication with the surface, a difficulty which did not trouble the helmeted diver, thanks to his tether, and to the fact that he did not receive his air supply through a mouth-piece. An answer was found by installing an underwater telephone booth, in the guise of an inverted dome, standing on legs, into which air-filled hemisphere a user could place his head and shoulders and speak freely into a microphone. The booth also served as a haven for a diver who found himself in trouble, and after one such incident, a spare air bottle was installed for use in an emergency. Yet another safety measure was the provision of a submersible decompression chamber, able to accommodate four men at a time, and kept anchored close to the site.

V

At Cape Gelidonya and Yassi Ada, for the first time, the scientific excavation of deep water sites was carried to completion

---

*First to receive attention was a nearby Roman ship, a century or so older than its Byzantine companion. But no sooner was the excavation of this vessel begun than the remains of a third were discovered lying across it. This unexpected find appeared to be of Islamic origin, dating from the time of the Crusades.

under the personal direction of a professional archaeologist. Moreover, in demonstrating the feasibility of such an undertaking, the operations not only provided graduate students with an opportunity to gain valuable diving experience, which they could afterwards put to use elsewhere,* but they led to the introduction of new techniques, and drew attention to a number of outstanding problems which still awaited a satisfactory solution.

The root cause of such difficulties may be regarded as twofold—the liquid medium in which investigators are called upon to work, and the strictly limited period of time they find themselves able to spend in the midst of this hostile environment. This last is a circumstance which not only tends unduly to prolong underwater excavation, but one which also precludes adequate supervision on the part of the leader, if all activity at the site is not to be restricted to less than one hour (in two stints) out of every 24. At Grand Congloué, non-diving archaeologists were able continuously to watch something of what was going on below on a television screen, but such an arrangement, in which the viewer cannot exercise control because he is helpless to intervene, must be as frustrating as the alternative prospect of making a descent to the scene of operations in a sealed observation chamber. Given, then, that the leader must be an archaeologist whose active participation is essential, even if his daily visits to the site are restricted to two or three brief appearances, his only answer, as things are, is to have resort to the not always satisfactory expedient of delegating his responsibilities.

As for the disadvantages of working in fluid surroundings, apart from this slowing down and adding to the difficulties of the task in all its aspects, most noticeable is the adverse effect it has on excavation and recording. In respect of the one, the investigator may well find himself faced by a highly unstable situation over which he can exercise a minimum of control. And as regards the other, he will almost certainly be greatly

*Thus the aforementioned Michael Katzev in due course transferred his attention from Yassi Ada to the remains of a Greek ship discovered in the vicinity of Kyrenia, Cyprus. Under his leadership, excavation was started in the summer of 1968, and among other items the vessel yielded a bronze coin minted in the lifetime of Alexander the Great. The (mainly Rhodian) amphorae which were recovered dated from the fourth century B.C. The hull, found to be in an excellent state of preservation, was also raised.

handicapped by water movement and turbidity, by disorientation caused by the lack of a horizon, and by distortion of vision, all combining to make the task of surveying and mapping both laborious and time-consuming, in circumstances where undue exertion needs to be avoided, and not a minute is to be wasted.

Where, then, to seek for remedies? In so far as extending the endurance of dives is concerned, the solution (discounting, for the moment, the possible creation of Cousteau's *Homo Aquaticus*) has already been found in the undersea dwelling. Thus housed, members of a community of archaeologists could work all the hours they wished (or at any rate of which they were capable) for weeks or months on end, if need be, eventually to face a single, if somewhat prolonged, period of decompression on leaving the water. Quite apart from the extension of working hours, the time saved by doing away with the necessity of undergoing repeated decompressions would also be considerable. Thus at Yassi Ada, where thousands of individual descents were made, a like number of ascents must have entailed a collective decompression period in excess of a thousand hours, all of which (until the S.D.C. arrived) the luckless divers spent dangling from the end of a rope, 10 feet below the surface!

As for surveying and mapping, an essential feature of any archaeological investigation, be it above water or below it, and both prior to and during the excavation of a site, is the keeping of detailed records, to be followed by their publication for the benefit of all who may have an interest in the undertaking. The fulfilment of this dual obligation is a tacit acknowledgement of the fact that digging is unavoidably accompanied by the obliteration of evidence which, once it has been lost, can never be recovered—though this is not to say, of course, that a satisfactory documentation is invariably achieved.

P. Courbin, in a recent editorial note (*Etude Archeologiques*, Paris, 1963) went so far as to express the view that, in the past, working conditions have often been such that 'they destroyed the answers before the questions could be posed', in consequence of which the results of excavation frequently turned out to be virtually useless for anything other than art history. No doubt there are many field archaeologists who would disagree with such a critical assessment of the outcome of their labours. But if this state of affairs can be said to exist where activities on land are concerned, what of operations which need to be conducted underwater, where the prevailing situation is even more unfavourable and exacting?

Any difference in working conditions between a dry and a wet dig is theoretically one of degree, in that the extent of the inundation may vary from a mere trickle of water to oceanic depths measurable in miles. However, in practice it is found that an underwater location may usually be identified as one or other of the two major items of archaeological interest earlier characterized as mobile or non-mobile, a distinction which arises, not only because drowned buildings and other permanent structures must originally have occupied positions at or near the water's edge, but also for the reason that a movable unit such as a wooden sailing vessel which foundered among shallows would, in the normal course of events, soon be broken up. To survive for any length of time, such a ship needs to settle amid surroundings which in addition to being sandy, are placed well beyond the reach of pounding waves and the no less destructive activities of salvors and plunderers.

From this, it follows that the nature of a site and the extent of its submersion—comparatively deep, if mobile, relatively slight, if non-mobile—govern the method of approach, and that where a site is located near the surface, the procedure adopted may well amount to little more than an extension of that used on land. Thus, in the case of ancient harbour foundations and the like, the depth of water (assuming it to be possessed of the requisite clarity) will allow a preliminary photographic mapping of the area from the air. When the extent and outlines of a site have been determined by this means, it will greatly facilitate the making of an architectural survey, as this is an undertaking in which one or more of a number of established methods can usefully be employed, as dictated by the exigencies of the situation. Thanks to the close proximity of the coast, triangulation with the aid of a land-based plane table and alidade, used in conjunction with ranging poles projecting above the surface of the water, offers no particular difficulty. And once the main outlines of a structural complex have been plotted, details of individual components can be sketched or photographed, and their dimensions ascertained by direct measurement.

Any subsequent excavation, preceded, if necessary, by clearing the site of marine growths, will serve both to reveal the full extent of the area under examination by the removal of mud and debris, and to ensure the recovery of any portable objects of interest this sedimentary accumulation may be found to contain. As for the making of a stratigraphical approach, while in certain situations the value of this may be open to question, it has nevertheless been shown to be an undertaking which presents no insuperable obstacles. In any event, should all else fail, and the circumstances be considered to justify the expense it would involve, a shallow location offers the advantage that it can be converted into a dry site by the removal of its aqueous surroundings. Such a procedure (though the circumstances were exceptional) has even been successfully carried out in respect of shipping, notably at Lake Nemi, and at Roskilde Fjord, in Denmark.

This last undertaking began as a conventional underwater operation, jointly headed by Olaf Olsen and Ole Crumlin-Pedersen of the National Museum, Copenhagen, in which divers equipped with aqualungs began the task of clearing away a mud and stone covering from a group of 5 Viking block ships, occupying a strategic position where they had lain undisturbed for the best part of a thousand years.

Progress, however, was interrupted and delayed by a combination of strong currents and bad visibility, which greatly hindered the making of a detailed plan of the site. In view of this, and assisted by the fact that in places the water was no more than 3 or 4 feet deep, it was eventually (1962) decided to surround the ships by a coffer dam (some 1,600 square yards in extent) and pump the enclosure dry. This was done, and as soon as the vessels were exposed to the air, they were cleaned by a spraying device, photographed where they lay, and their crumbling timbers tagged, lifted, and stored in plastic bags, as a prelude to immersion in polyethylene glycol. The importance of the enterprise as an exercise in underwater archaeology lies in the fact that it provides one of the few instances in which the remains of ancient ships have been reclaimed from the sea, and in such a manner as to permit of their reconstruction. But without in any way seeking to detract from this outstanding achievement, it will be evident that the method by which it was accomplished is not applicable to a deep water site.

And yet, at any rate in theory, there is a simple variation of the coffer dam technique which could be used in such a situation, thanks to the circumstance that, by definition, portable objects would be involved, i.e., objects of limited size, ranging from a solitary anchor to a fully-laden amphora carrier. And in the case of an item such as the last-named, calling not merely for retrieval, but for a detailed on-the-spot investigation, a sufficiently large dome, either prefabricated or erected *in situ*, could be placed over the site and the water it contained forced out by pumping in air. Since the atmosphere thus introduced would automatically adjust itself to the prevailing water pressure, the structure could be of relatively light construction. It would, of course, be necessary for the rim of the hemisphere to rest on a flat base, a requirement which, on sloping or uneven ground, would have to be met by levelling the sea-bed, while holding the structure down against the upward thrust of the imprisoned air would be no easy task. But the provision of dry, or near dry, working conditions, would appear to be the ultimate answer to many of the problems at present associated with underwater excavation, especially as it would enable those engaged in the task to take up residence at the site.

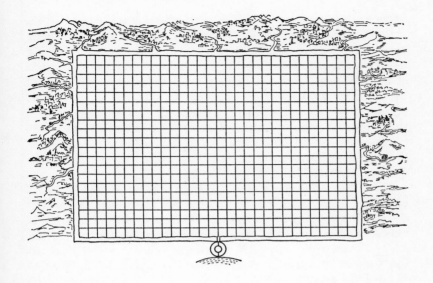

Chapter Eight

Lost Lands and Submerged Cities

I

Reports about vanished lands and drowned cities, supposedly engulfed by the rising waters of the sea, tend to be regarded somewhat askance by men of science—and not without good reason. Geologically, all such accounts are as highly suspect as they are chronologically awry, in that no significant alteration in ocean levels would appear to have taken place during the past 6,000 years, at the start of which period even the most advanced representatives of mankind were still in the throes of the Stone Age. Thus, on the face of it, the time factor alone provides sufficient justification for the dismissal of such colourful tales as those of the lost continents of Atlantis, and of its Pacific and Indian Ocean equivalents, Lemuria and Mu.

In so far as the legendary Atlantis is concerned, there is no convincing evidence whatsoever to support the thesis that a highly civilized, if warlike, island community flourished beyond the confines of the Mediterranean (and yet within striking distance of Athens) some 10,000 years ago—even assuming that the Greek city then took the form of anything more than a primitive Neolithic settlement. As for the origins of this unlikely story, it will be recollected that it was retailed by Plato,[107] who inherited it from his illustrious predecessor Solon (c. 600 B.C.) who in turn obtained his information from the priests of Sais, in Egypt. This was to the effect that, as a punishment for the impiety of their attack upon the Athenians, the aggressors and their island home were smitten by earthquakes and swallowed up by the sea.

Notwithstanding that in the light of modern knowledge and enquiry, the fictional content of the narrative clearly exceeds the factual, a belief in the onetime existence of Plato's Atlantis persists to this day, as is evidenced by the recent republication (in 1960 and 1962, respectively) of the literary outpourings on the subject of such nineteenth century apostles as Ignatius Donnelly[47] and W. Scott-Elliot.[123] Suffice it to say that the Donnelly work associates the destruction of Atlantis with the Noachian Deluge, and that in an editorial aside, the reader is solemnly admonished that a denial of the one event would automatically imply a disbelief in the other—as well it might; the credibility of pentateuchal accounts of the Flood, alas, no longer commands an unqualified acceptance on the part of biblical scholars. As for Scott-Elliot, who casually refers to a time 'about a million years ago, when the Atlantean race was at its height', his oracularities are addressed to those in whom 'the faculties are sufficiently enlarged to enter into concise relationship with the superphysical planes or aspects of Nature'.

All this is plainly nonsense of an esoteric and lofty order, and in days gone by it has been accompanied by much profitless speculation concerning the precise location of the now vanished island. A site much favoured in the past has been that occupied by the Azores which, it was claimed, were the mountain peaks of Atlantis, a view seemingly endorsed by the discovery, made during cable laying, of the existence of an extensive mid-Atlantic ridge. And as recently as 1955 a German advocate, Otto H. Muck,[98] furnished additional arguments in support of this particular theory. He reasoned that when Atlantis suffered catastrophic destruction (in the year 9564 B.C., according to Scott-Elliot!), a land barrier was removed which permitted an eastward flow of the Gulf Stream, as a result of which its warm waters hastened the ending of Europe's last glacial period, albeit their change of course did not alter the life cycle of the eel, which creatures instinctively retained their age-old rendezvous with the Sargasso Sea: they could not forget Atlantis. Unfortunately, there is an insuperable obstacle to the proposed identification of the Azores or, indeed, of any other part of the Atlantic, as the site of the missing continent. Core samples taken from the ocean floor have provided incontrovertible proof, in the guise of undisturbed sedimentary deposits and rock strata, that relevant areas of the sea-bed have been continuously under water for millions of years.

But although the Platonic narrative thus stands discredited in terms of both time and place, this is not to say that it is not amenable to a less literal interpretation. Not a few superficially fanciful myths and legends have been shown, on close investigation, to have been inspired by events, the exact details of which have long since been forgotten—the biblical account of the Deluge, for instance, provides a case in point. The composite (and somewhat contradictory) account given in Genesis, of a flood which engulfed the entire surface of the earth, is clearly a fabrication in which the highly improbable vies with the downright impossible. Moreover, not merely is the story of Noah fictitious, but it cannot even claim the merit of originality: it has been convincingly shown to be a Hebraic borrowing from the Babylonians, who in turn acquired it from the Sumerians. As to what inspired this extravagant tale about angry gods who arbitrarily decide to bring about the wholesale elimination of mankind by drowning, the answer is to be found in the geography of the land of ancient Sumer, essentially an alluvial plain across which flowed the Tigris and Euphrates Rivers. Since time immemorial, both these waterways have been subject to flooding as their lower reaches, swollen by melting snow from the highlands of Asia Minor, a thousand miles distant, reached a peak level in April (Tigris) and May (Euphrates), a phenomenon which continues to this day, as witness the widespread inundation of the region which occurred in 1954.

On the evidence of historic references, it would appear that one such incident was so catastrophic in its effects that it came to be known as *the* flood. Thus the following mention, preceded by a listing of the names of 5 cities and those of 8 antediluvian monarchs, was recorded by a local scribe:

> The flood came. After the flood had come, kingship again came down from on high. The kingship was at Kish. . . .

Archaeological investigations in Mesopotamia (Gk., 'The Land between the Rivers') not only brought to light written statements such as this, but they revealed the existence of extensive accumulations of water-borne silt at the sites of a number of ancient cities. The tell-tale layers of sediment were variously dated from 2800 B.C. (by Stephen H. Langden, at Kish) to 3000–4000 B.C. (by Leonard Woolley, at Ur), and thus provided evidence of more than one instance of serious flooding in the distant past. At Ur, the water-laid mud was between 8 and 11 feet thick, and analysis showed that it had been brought down by the Euphrates. The accompanying deluge was, of course, no more than a local phenomenon, but Woolley[149] estimated the depth of water to have been not less than twenty-five feet, sufficient to cover the whole of the territory extending from the Elamite mountains in the east to the elevated Syrian desert in the west, an area of some 30,000 square miles. Small wonder, then, that an occurrence such as this made a lasting impression upon the mind of Mesopotamian man.

The question thus arises as to whether the Atlantis myth is similarly explicable in terms of a natural disaster of such vast and terrifying proportions that it became a folk-memory which ultimately attained its present discredited form by a gradual process of amendment and elaboration. And a possible answer has been found in the rapid decline of the Minoan civilization which took place about 1400 B.C. More than 30 years ago, T. Frost drew attention to certain similarities between the Bronze Age Cretans and the Atlanteans, who were also said to have made extensive use of the alloy, a correlation which has recently been endorsed by Spyridon Marinatos, of the Department of Antiquities, at Athens. A. G. Galanopoulos thereupon undertook a study of Atlantean measurements, as recorded by Plato, and reached the remarkable conclusion that these had been overstated by a factor of ten—possibly because of an inadvertent reading of the Egyptian glyph for 100 as 1,000 on the part of Solon. In effect, not only was the size of the kingdom grossly exaggerated, *but so was the time said to have elapsed since the date of the catastrophe.* Chronological credibility, that is to say, could be conferred upon the narrative by making the

35. *The extent of Minoan (Atlantean?) civilisation at the time of the destruction of the island of Santorin, c. 1450 B.C. (after Myres, Ninkovich, and Heezen).*

assumption that the destruction of Atlantis occurred, not 9,000, but 900, years before Solon's day, so bringing the event within the Minoan period. In short, the Atlanteans were to be identified with the Cretans, whose kingdom extended to the mainland of the eastern Mediterranean, and included the intervening islands. As for the geographic discrepancy, it needs to be remembered, as J. L. Myres[100] pointed out some years ago, that the rise and fall of the Minoan civilization were events completely outside the knowledge of the Greek historians of the classical period. Galanopoulos accordingly supposes that by the time Plato received the story of Atlantis, enough was known about the islands of the Mediterranean for him to realize that none was sufficiently large to meet the requirements of the much magnified story, the location of which was hopefully transferred to the mysterious vastness of the unexplored Atlantic Ocean.

36. Present-day remnants of the volcanic island of Santorin (after H. Reck and others).

There remains the destruction of the Mediterranean Atlantis, and the manner in which it came about, an event which has been associated with a violent disturbance which, *c.* 1450 B.C. is known to have caused the near obliteration of the former island of Stronghyli (otherwise Santorin) which is now represented by disjoined remnants individually identified as the islands of Thera, Aspronisi, and Therasia, together with the Kamenis, which rose from the sea in 197 B.C. Some 70 miles separated this Cretan settlement from Crete itself, both of whose leading towns and ports would have been wiped out by the catastrophic eruption—those of the one by a gigantic

explosion accompanied by earthquakes, the coastal communities of the other by a succession of giant waves which
followed in the wake of the Stronghyli disaster.*

While such an explanation may offer some prospect of
vindicating Plato, it is manifestly not one that can be used to
sustain the notion that counterparts of Atlantis were once to
be found in the midst of the Pacific and Indian Oceans: the
existence of the now supposedly lost continents of Lemuria and
Mu is simply not in accord with the geological facts.

II

Yet another expanse of territory widely believed to have been
lost to the encroaching sea is that which is once said to have
linked Cornwall with the Isles of Scilly—the fabled Land of
Lyonesse (Lennoys or Leonais), to which an early reference
occurs in association with the Arthurian legend. Mention of a
drowned land which used to extend from St. Michael's Mount
to the Scillies is to be found in the *Itinerary of William of Worcester*,
a fifteenth century Latin prose work. And round this account of
a once fertile and populated region, containing no less than
140 parishes, there gathered the usual tales about the solitary
survivor who escaped a sudden and devastating inundation
by galloping for his life astride a white charger, since when the
sound of seven score church bells can occasionally be heard, as
they peal in concert beneath the waves in stormy weather. Or
so it is said.

Seemingly, it was left to a resident antiquarian, Richard
Carew[16] of East Antony, positively to associate Cornwall with
the lost Land of Lyonesse, which he did in a collection of local
traditions (of somewhat dubious historical worth) first published
in 1602. After lamenting the inroads upon his native territory
which had been made in the tenth century by the invading
King Athelstan, he goes on:

*To refer to these waves as tidal is an obvious, if popular, misnomer. In coastal
regions, movements of water caused by severe earth tremors often inflict more
damage and destruction than the quakes themselves, on occasion giving rise to
waves 100 feet high which sweep landwards at speeds in excess of 400 miles an
hour. The Japanese, to whom such incidents are all too familiar an experience, have
a special name for the phenomenon—*Tsunami* (Jap. *tsu*, harbour, *nami*, waves)—
which seismologists have adopted. The word represents both the singular and the
plural form.

13

Lastly, the encroaching sea hath ravined from it the whole country of Lyonesse, together with divers other parcels of no little circuit, and that such a Lyonesse there was these proofs are yet remaining. The space between the Land's End and the Isles of Scilly, being about thirty miles, to this day retaineth the name, in Cornish *Lethowsow*, and carry continually at an equal depth for forty or sixty fathom (a thing not usual in the sea's proper dominion) save that about the midway there lieth a rock which at low water discovereth its head.

The geology of the region, as already noted in connection with the submerged Stone Age implement factory discovered in the vicinity of Mounts Bay, indicates that in the course of centuries, the land has sunk by as much as 40 feet or more. The intervening terrain, however, would need to have subsided to an extent far in excess of this figure to account for the maximum depth of water which now separates the Scilly Isles

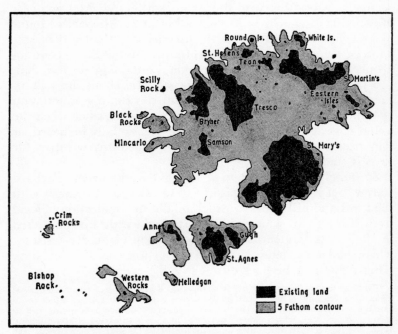

37. *The Isles of Scilly, showing the contour of the 5 fathom line (after Dunbar).*

from the mainland, so that the time when a peninsulate connection may have existed between the two places recedes into
the remote and unrecorded past.

The conclusion thus seems inescapable that Lyonesse did not
constitute a seaward extension of Cornwall, at any rate in
historic times, and that if it existed at all, it must have been as a
land cut off by water, a domain whose mountain peaks can
hardly have been other than the six main islands and the
hundred and more rocky islets which go to make up the
Scillies. As to this, some years ago H. O'Neill Hencken[70]
pointed out that if the present ten fathom mark be taken to
represent the ancient shore line, all the members of the group
become hills on one large island, with an area of some 50
square miles. Similarly, and more recently, John Dunbar[53]
has shown that even if a relatively modest subsidence of no
more than 30 feet be assumed to have taken place, the contour
of the five fathom line produces a map on which all the large
islands are joined together, with the exception of St. Agnes.

As it happens, this idea of former unition is by no means
new. More than two centuries ago, the Reverend Dr. William
Borlase[12] observed what he took to be evidence of it, as he duly
noted when communicating his findings to the Dean of Exeter.
After making mention of Trescaw (Tresco), Brehar (Bryher),
and Sampson (Samson), he added:

> Thefe are certain evidences that the Iflands laft mentioned were
> once one continued tract of Land, divided into Fields, and
> cultivated even in thofe low parts which are now over-run with
> Sea and the Sand.

Among the evidences in question, Borlase cited 'Hedges of
ftone . . . running many feet under the level of the Sea', whose
existence and ostensible purpose were subsequently confirmed
by an archaeologist associated with the Ordnance Survey.
O. G. S. Crawford, who made his examination in the 1920s,
was assisted in his task by exceptionally low tides and by the
then novel technique of aerial photography, of which he was one
of the pioneers. His investigations convinced him that the stone
walls were undoubtedly human handiwork, a view afterwards
endorsed by Professor Hencken, who also drew attention to the
implications of certain other walls, standing

on small islands that not have neither fresh water nor inhabitants. One of these is on Old Man, and divides a point of the
island now so small that it was obviously built when there was
much more land.

However, the conclusion that the Isles of Scilly offered
conclusive evidence of land subsidence in the shape of inundated fields was later (1949) challenged on the score that the
walled areas in question bore a remarkable resemblance to a
type of South African fish trap, at which point the aforementioned John Dunbar, an archaeologist by profession and a diver
by inclination, organized what has been claimed to be the first
underwater investigation of its kind to be carried out in
Britain.

The dozen or so members of his 1956 Scillies expedition were
fully equipped with aqualungs, face masks, protective suits, and
all the other accessories of the modern free diver, and in addition
to the submerged hedges of stone, it was proposed to investigate
persistent reports (at least from the time of Borlase onwards)
of the existence of paved roads which had once connected the
various islands. But apart from traces of rubble of an in-
determinate nature which were located in the shallows between
Tresco and St. Martins, no signs of the alleged causeways could
be found, and this despite diligent searching. As for the underwater walling, Dunbar reached the considered conclusion
that in some instances at least, it might well have been designed
and built in order to steer fast running fish, coming in on the
tide, in a particular and desired direction.

Disappointingly, in so far as the question of land sinkage was
concerned, the evidence obtained was no more conclusive than
that to be derived from the existence on the hilltops of the
islands of a disproportionately high number of Bronze Age
burial mounds, having regard for the paucity of habitations
dating from the same period. This is a circumstance which is
capable of more than one explanation. To some investigators it
suggests that these high and isolated places were used by the
people of the mainland for the interment of their dead chief-
tains, in which event inundation may, or may not, have
subsequently occurred. Alternatively, there is the possibility
that the remains of the missing dwellings are to be found in
what may prove to be the now drowned valleys which separate

the islands. But even supposing this to be the case, the legend of
Lyonesse has then to be reconciled with a land subsidence which
apparently took place some 4,000 years ago! In the light of this,
as O. G. S. Crawford has remarked, the probability would
seem to be that the story of lost territory to the south-west of
Cornwall, far from being based on the memory of an actual
event, merely represents a much more recent attempt to explain
the presence in the Scillies of what was otherwise to be regarded
as the inexplicability of submarine walling.

III

More credible than tales of lost lands and vanished continents
are accounts of drowned cities and sunken harbours, and while
it may be safely assumed that the foundations of the last-named
have laid submerged since the day they were built, other
non-mobile structures (such as houses and streets) have clearly
come to be under water by accident—if not gradually, thanks
to a slow and almost imperceptible settlement on the part of the
land upon which they stood, then abruptly, as the result of some
violent upheaval. In either case, it is likely that silting will
afterwards have taken place, and that this will have obscured
the site, wholly or in part, thus adding to the difficulties of
locating and investigating it. On the other hand, whereas a

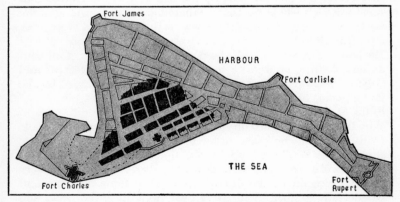

*38. Plan of Port Royal. The dark area (within the dotted line) shows
that part of the town which remained above water after the earthquake of
1692 (based on a contemporary print).*

prolonged process of submergence, extending over many decades, may well have excited little notice or comment, the sudden and catastrophic inundation of a port or city in historic times would almost certainly be a matter of record, and such documentation, if still extant, could provide an invaluable guide to the whereabouts of any remains.

An example of this is provided by the almost total destruction of a harbour town on the southern coast of Jamaica, a comparatively recent disaster which happens to be particularly well attested. The devastated town, afterwards to be replaced by nearby Kingston, was sited at the end of a long, low and curving sandspit, known as the Palisadoes, which terminated in a small island. Here, seventeenth century British emigrants filled in the intervening marshland and established a settlement which they named Port Royal. Thereafter, although the region was periodically subjected to minor earth tremors, no damage of any consequence was sustained until 7 June, 1692, when it seemed to the town's inhabitants that the end of the world had come. According to the report of one eyewitness:

> The morning of this dreadful day was very fair and clear, affording no suspicion of the least evil, but in the space of three minutes about half an hour after eleven in the morning, *Port Royal* . . . was shaken and shattered to pieces and sunk into and covered for the greatest part by the sea. Few of the Houses that stood were left whole. So that by them falling, the opening of the Earth and the inundation of the waters, it is reckoned there were loft fifteen hundred Persons . . . It was a sad sight to see all that Harbour . . . covered with the dead bodies of People of all conditions, floating up and down without burial, for the great and famous Burial-place called the Pallisadoes, was destroyed by the Earthquake, of which there were hundreds in that place . . . From *St. Anns* there was news that above a thousand acres of Woodland were turned into the sea and carried with it whole Plantations, but no place suffered like *Port Royal*, where whole streets were swallowed up by the opening of the Earth, and Houses and Inhabitants went down together. Some of them were driven up again by the Sea which arose in those breaches and wonderfully escaped. Some were swallowed up to the neck, and then the Earth shut upon them and squeezed them to death, and in that manner several were left buried, with their heads above the ground, only Some Heads the Dogs had eaten . . .

Other contemporary accounts describe how three violent quakes took place in rapid succession, to be followed by a great wave which snapped the cables of ships at anchor in the harbour (the frigate *Swan* was swept inland and flung on to some rooftops) and brought ruin and destruction to everything in its path. When the flood waters receded, all that remained of the town was confined to a small area of land, now again an island, while of Forts Carlisle and James, nothing was to be seen. Some of the other wrecked buildings stood partly immersed, half in and half out of the water, in which situation they long remained, while many were completely submerged, covered by the sea to a depth of between 25 and 50 feet.

For several decades following the disaster, much salvaging of valuables was undertaken with the aid of diving bells, but gradually the ruins sank, and in the course of so doing, became covered with sediment, the steady deposition of which re-established the land connection with the Palisadoes. This silting-up process has since continued, and although until about a century ago it was still possible to discern some of the sunken buildings, in 1907 another severe earthquake toppled many of the walls that had remained standing, soon after which most of the newly fallen structures vanished beneath a carpet of mud.

This was the situation Edwin Link found when he brought *Sea Diver* to Port Royal in 1958, where he was confronted by what was virtually an untouched site. Archaeologically, of course, it held promise of few surprises, but after carrying out a preliminary survey, in the course of which he retrieved an old cannon, Link expressed himself as satisfied that the place merited his attention. Accordingly, this time on board the recently commissioned *Sea Diver II*, he returned to Jamaica in the following year accompanied by a dozen or so divers, amongst whom were to be found the Smithsonian Institute's Mendel Peterson and representatives of the National Geographic Society.

An immediate problem which faced the investigators was the lack of clarity of the water, which was overcome by employing an echo sounder, used in conjunction with old maps of the area. In this manner, the position of the two vanished forts was established, which in turn enabled the outlines of intermediate buildings to be plotted and buoyed. At a selected

spot alongside the east wall of Fort James, an air-lift was installed and set to burrowing into a layer of mud which proved
to be ten feet in thickness, by which time the pipe's surface
outlet was spewing forth a stream of minor artifacts ranging
from silver spoons and clay pipes to onion-shaped rum bottles.
At the intake end, meanwhile, working in a dense and im-
penetrable cloud of mud, the divers recovered an assortment
of other items, among them cooking pots, cannon balls, and a
fifteenth century swivel gun of Spanish manufacture. But the
most informative find was a brass watch, dating from the 1680s,
whose maker was one Paul Blondel, of Amsterdam. Although it
had lost its hands, the position at which these had stopped was
ascertained by radiographic means, and shown to be 17 minutes
to 12, thus fixing the time of the disaster.

Edwin Link's interest inevitably served to draw attention to
the site, and after his departure, other divers arrived and there
soon developed an illicit trade involving the sale and smuggling
of artifacts. A governmental decision to discourage such activities by sponsoring an official investigation was hastened by the
discovery that a group of American visitors, whose yacht was
fitted with an underwater hatch, had managed to pilfer the sea-
bed for some months before the secret of their unseen comings
and goings was revealed by a chance encounter in the muddy
depths. The offenders were requested to leave, and in 1965,
the post of marine archaeologist was offered to, and accepted
by, the diver Robert Marx.[94]

Although Marx and his team began by making a methodical
examination of a designated area of the harbour floor, buoying
and plotting the position of each find, in view of the slow
progress this entailed, it was decided to install an air-lift.
The disposal of sediment at once became a problem, for the
area under investigation was so extensive that if the silt had
been discharged into the water, and left to be carried away by
the current, it would inevitably have settled on some other part
of the site. Accordingly, a barge was used to collect the stream
of muddy water and artifacts, and the unwanted debris
periodically dumped overboard at some barren spot.

Marx had proposed to make a strictly stratigraphical
approach, excavating layer by layer within a measured
square of aluminium tubing. This intention was frustrated,

however, on the one hand by the circumstance that the sea-bed had been, and was still being, ploughed up by the dragging of anchors, and on the other by the discovery that as the excavation deepened, its sides displayed an unpreventable tendency to collapse. Heavy rains, by bringing down fresh supplies of mud, added to the difficulties of the divers, but despite such interruptions (including a minor earthquake), scores of artifacts were recovered, not least a crumbling wooden chest containing hundreds of coins, dating from 1653 to 1690. A plaque on the chest bearing a coat of arms proclaimed its rightful owner to have been the Spanish Crown.

Even more important was the finding of a collection of thousands of items marking the grave of a sunken ship, included among which were two lead draught markers in the guise of the Roman numerals VII and IX (or XI), which suggested that the vessel must have been of considerable size. Of the ship itself, only the keel, ribs, and parts of the lower deck were discovered, buried beneath six feet of mud, not to mention a section of brick wall. Various signs convinced the investigators that the remains were those of a warship, the British nationality of which was indicated by markings in the shape of a broad arrow. As Admiralty records showed that only one such British vessel had been lost in the disaster of 1692, it appeared to be a reasonable deduction that the wreck was that of the ill-fated *Swan* which, after being tossed inland, had evidently accompanied its stricken surroundings as they gradually subsided beneath the sea.

IV

Historic accounts and chance finds have between them led to searches for, or investigations of, not a few drowned communities in various parts of the world, from those of Sodom and Gomorrha, long ago swallowed up by the waters of the Dead Sea,* to the Kirghiz district of the Soviet Republic,

---

*Where, it needs always to be remembered, diving in waters whose salinity is five times greater than that of the ocean, demands special precautions. Not only does the high density of the water entail greatly increased air consumption, but its extreme buoyancy makes essential the use of heavy lead weights as sinkers. These, moreover, must be capable of gradual release, lest in discarding them, the wearer should shoot to the surface before he has had time to empty his over-expanded lungs.

where members of an expedition to Lake Issyk-Kul discovered, on a now submerged central island, the structural remains of the fortress prison built by Timur-I-Lenk (Timur the Lame— Tamerlane), and destroyed by an earthquake in recent times (fifteenth century, A.D.).

As in the case of ancient shipwrecks, however, the most likely place to seek underwater edificial remains is without doubt the Mediterranean, not only because many of the early civilizations had access to its shores, but also because the region is almost entirely enclosed by mountains which, geologically, are of recent origin. In consequence, the surrounding terrain is still highly unstable and in the process of adjusting itself to the stresses and strains which attended its formation, as is evidenced by a long and continuing history of volcanic eruptions and earth tremors, accompanied by compensatory movements involving the periodic rise or fall of considerable stretches of the coastline. This combination of high density population and crustal instability is reflected in some surprising statistics. According to the researches of N. F. Flemming,[43] in the years from 3000 B.C. to the end of the Roman Empire, more than 300 major ports and cities were built at or near the water's edge, interspersed with countless fishing villages and residential villas, fully half of all of which have since become submerged, wholly or in part.

By the middle of the present century, many of these sites had been investigated, thanks to the pioneer efforts of such enthusiasts as Guiseppe de Fazio, Robert Theodore Gunther, Gaston Jondet, and Antione Poidebard, and the work has since been continued by others, at places as widely separated Cherchel and Salamis (in Algeria and Cyprus), Carthage and Caesarea (in Tunisia and Palestine), Apollonia and Fos-sur-Mer (in Libya and France). Thus at Fos, west of Marseilles, members of a team of volunteer divers (*Societe des Amis due vieil Istres*), working under professional guidance, have been excavating the remains of a Roman settlement now lying under fifteen feet of water. Believed to mark the site of the ancient port of Fosses-de-Marius, the remains of one villa have been uncovered which yielded a fine collection of pottery and other household items, including a small votive altar which was discovered surrounded by its lamps.

39. Reconstruction of the ancient Greek port of Apollonia, in Cyrenaica, whose submerged remains were investigated by members of the 1958–59 Cambridge University Expedition (based on an original drawing by Judy Hannington).

At Apollonia, in Cyrenaica (not to be confused with other towns of the same name in Chalcidice, Illyria, Mygdonia, Palestine, Sicily, or Thrace), N. F. Flemming[43] and a group of Cambridge University students devoted two seasons (1958–9) to making a detailed survey of the partly drowned remains of the Greek city, with a view to determining the date and the cause of its inundation. It was found that rather more than half the ruined site is now under water, and that it was originally fronted by a complex of inner and outer harbours, protected by an extensive system of breakwaters, and replete with 10 slipways, each 23 feet wide, 92 feet long, with an incline of 4 degrees. The depth of water at the foot of the slopes was slightly more than 9 feet, greatly in excess of that needed to take the keels of even the largest vessels of the time (*c*. 500 B.C.). This, coupled with the discovery of a large submerged fish tank, once connected to the sea by a series of sluiced channels, provided evidence of a rise in water level (due to land subsidence) of more than 6 feet. A recent geological survey of the area, which disclosed the existence of minor dislocations, suggests that the settlement was caused by local faulting. As to the date of the occurrence, although there is no reason to suppose that it was other than gradual, it may have been associated with an earthquake known to have devastated nearby Cyrene in the fourth century A.D.

The last season of the Apollonia investigations chanced to coincide with the arrival of Edwin Link and *Sea Diver II* at Haifa, *en route* for the site of Caesarea, a few miles along the coast. Named in honour of Augustus Caesar by its builder, Herod the Great of Judea (37–4 B.C.), in its heyday it was the only harbour which offered sheltered port facilities in the whole of Palestine, and it prospered accordingly. The historian Josephus, who visited the city within a century of the death of Herod, recounted how that monarch had provided it with an anchorage which always offered protection from the great waves of the sea, thanks to the construction of a semicircular jetty. The harbour's northern entrance ('from where blew the weakest of all the winds of this region') was flanked on either side by three giant statues of polished stone—long since vanished, it needs hardly to be said.

An aerial reconnaisance enabled Link to trace the outlines of the now submerged harbour walls, which proved to be circular on the south side, but straight on the north, with a gap showing between the tips of the two converging arms. An air-lift, used to move a deep accumulation of sand which had lodged against the sides of these structures, at first produced nothing, but at a depth of sixteen feet a multitude of artifacts began to be uncovered—amphorae, pottery, ivory hairpins, bronze nails, coins by the score. No doubt what Link had very much in mind were the outsize statues which had once stood guard at the harbour entrance, but although none of these figures was found, his efforts did produce evidence of their onetime existence. This was provided by the finding of a solitary tessera, on which Caesarea was depicted, complete with the stone colossi and a pair of Roman galleys—the only known pictorial representation of the port in existence.

V

Thus far, and understandably enough, the interest of archaeologists in submerged ruins has been confined to sites whose whereabouts are known, and whose remains are visible (at any rate in part), are reasonably accessible, and are not too extensive in area. But what, in the days ahead, is likely to be their attitude to a site which offers no such inducements to the investigator, in that its exact location and extent have yet to be determined, and that in addition to lying under water, it is completely hidden from view by a thick deposit of mud?

By all accounts, such is the plight of the now vanished Greek city of Helice, evidence of the one-time existence of which, however, was unwittingly provided by Homer[75] when he compiled his catalogue of forces which assembled against Troy. Details of its location, moreover, and of the manner of its end, are given by Pausanias.[104] His reference concerns Achaia, in the Peloponnese:

> As you go on you come to the river Selinus, and about 40 stadia from Aegium is a place called Helice near the sea. It was once an important city, and the Ionians had there the most holy temple of Poseidon of Helice. The worship of Poseidon of Helice still remained with them, both when they were driven out by the Achaeans to Athens, and when they afterwards went from Athens to the maritime parts of Asia Minor . . .
>
> And later on the Achaeans here, who drove some suppliants from the temple and slew them, met with quick vengeance from Poseidon, for an earthquake coming over the place rapidly overthrew all the buildings, and made the very site of the city difficult for posterity to find. . . .
>
> And they say another misfortune happened to the place in the winter at the same time. The sea encroached over much of the district and quite flooded Helice with water: and the grove of Poseidon was so submerged that the tops of the trees alone were visible. And so the god suddenly sending the earthquake, and the sea encroaching simultaneously, the inundation swept away Helice and its population.

The date of the event has been provided by Strabo,[128] who explicitly states that the city was overwhelmed by the waves 'two years before the Battle of Leuctra'. This encounter between the Theban General Epaminondas and the Spartans, whom he decisively defeated, took place in 371 B.C., so making 373 B.C. the year of the catastrophe, a reckoning in accord with the assertion of Heracleidas of Pontus that the inundation happened in his time, i.e., prior to 322 B.C. Strabo also quotes Eratosthenes (c. 276–194 B.C.) as saying that he himself visited the scene of the disaster, and that the boatmen who ferried him over the spot informed him that, standing in the midst of the drowned ruins, there could formerly be seen a massive bronze statue of Poseidon, holding aloft a hippocampus.

The archaeological possibilities of Helice so interested the well known Hellenist R. Demangel (then stationed at Athens)

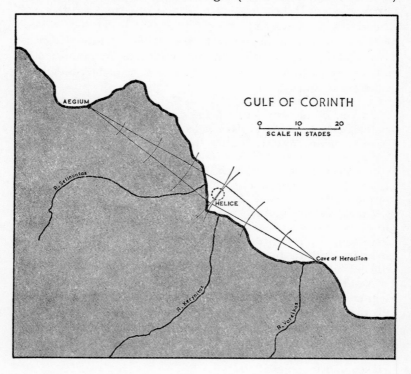

40. The whereabouts of the submerged city of Helice, reputedly located "40 stades from Aegium and 30 stades from the Cave of Heraclion".

that in 1950 he prevailed upon a group of French underwater swimmers to make an examination of the site. The four-man team was headed by Dr. Henri Chénevée, a dental surgeon by profession, and well known to members of the diving community as a somewhat colourful character who was imbued, among other things, with the notion that he was immune to nitrogen narcosis, thanks to his constant breathing of nitrous oxide while anaesthetizing his patients.

The situation found by Chénevée and his companions was far from encouraging. The sea in the neighbourhood of the drowned city was heavily impregnated with silt brought down by two rivers, and visibility was badly affected. But what finally persuaded the searchers to abandon their task was the discovery of a modern wreck (a victim of World War II) which, in the course of a single decade, had become almost entirely enveloped in mud. From this it was concluded that the rate of deposition which prevailed in the area left small hope of their happening upon signs of any structural remains which had been submerged for more than 2,000 years.

Having regard for all the difficulties which would un-doubtedly attend the making of a detailed investigation of such a site, it may well be enquired on what grounds the undertaking could possibly be justified. In the words of an unenthusiastic Honor Frost:[60]

> Why should archaeologists, at vast expense, examine sub-merged towns when so many land sites cry out for excavation?

The answer (as the questioner in effect concedes) is that each case needs to be considered on its merits, in which event the claim of Helice to receive attention may be adjudged particu-larly strong. Here, there is every reason to suppose, are to be found the remains of an entire community, whose buildings and their contents were suddenly and dramatically tumbled to the ground, and then engulfed by the sea. At the very least, the remnants of a unique collection of works of art dating from the fourth century B.C. await a finder, though the pleasing vision conjured up by Demangel, when he likened the ruins to an underwater Pompeii, would appear to offer investigators a prospect more daunting than inviting, when it is remembered that the relatively easy task of clearing the Roman town of its covering of volcanic tuff has now been going on, more or less continuously, for more than two hundred years—and has yet to be completed!

The crucial question, it would seem, is not whether the Helice undertaking is to be regarded as worthwhile, but whether or not it can be considered feasible. Much, of course, will depend upon the actual conditions which surround the site, assuming that a preliminary exploration confirms its existence. According to Demangel's estimate, the ruins are to be found at a distance of between 550 and 1,600 yards from the present shore-line, covered by a depth of water which varies from 50 to 130 feet, whereas N. C. Flemming[43] has hopefully conjectured that no more than 20 feet of water is likely to be encountered, plus an equal depth of mud. These estimations, it is to be suspected, rely heavily on guesswork, and only when the facts of the situation have been established can the prospects of carrying out a successful excavation be assessed. If the depth of water is as modest as Flemming suggests, then the provision of a coffer dam may well prove to be the ultimate and time-saving answer, as it would enable much of the mud and slime to be pumped out of the enclosure in a semi-liquid state.

Bibliography

1. Anderson, E. M., *The Dynamics of Faulting* (Oliver and Boyd, London, 1942).
2. Aristotle, *De Partibus Animalium* (Oxford University Press, London, 1912).
3. Aristotle, *Problemata* (Oxford University Press, London, 1927).
4. Bacon, F., *Novum Organum* (Bell and Daldy, London, 1859).
5. Baikie, J., *Egyptian Antiquities in the Nile Valley* (Methuen and Co. Ltd., London, 1932).
6. Balder, A. P., *The Complete Manual of Skin Diving* (Collier–Macmillan Ltd., London, 1968).
7. Barker, T. F., *Roman Galley Beneath the Sea* (Brockhampton Press, Leicester, 1964).
8. Barnes, H., *Oceanography and Marine Biology* (George Allen and Unwin Ltd., London, 1959).
9. Bass, G. F., *Archaeology Under Water* (Thames and Hudson, London, 1966).
10. Beiser, A., *The Earth* (Time–Life International [Nederland] N.V., 1964).
11. Bert, P., *Barometric Pressure* (College Book Company, Columbus, Ohio).
12. Borlase, W., *Observations on the Ancient and Prefent State of the Isles of Scilly* (W. Jackson, Oxford, 1756).
13. Bourlière, F., *Mammals of the World* (George Harrap and Co. Ltd., London, 1955).
14. Boutan, L., *La Photographie Sous-Marine* (Schleider Frères, Paris, 1900).
15. Bullard, F. M., *Volcanoes* (University of Texas Press, Austin, 1962).
16. Carew, R., *The Survey of Cornwall* (Andrew Melrose, London, 1953).
17. Carne, J., *Syria, The Holy Land and Asia Minor* (Fisher, Son and Co., London, 1836).
18. Carson, R. L., *The Sea Around Us* (Staples Press Ltd., London, 1951).

19. Cassius Dion, *Roman History* (William Heinemann, London, 1914).
20. Casson, L., *The Ancient Mariners* (Victor Gollancz Ltd., London, 1959).
21. Casteret, N., *Ten Years Under the Earth* (J. M. Dent and Sons Ltd., London, 1939).
22. Cayce, E. E., *Edgar Cayce on Atlantis* (Howard Baker Publishers Ltd., London, 1969).
23. Cayford, J. E., *Underwater Work* (Cornell Maritime Press Inc., Cambridge, U.S.A.).
24. Ceram, C. W., Ed., *The World of Archaeology* (Thames and Hudson, London, 1966).
25. Cervé, W. S., *Lemuria* (The Rosicrucian Press Ltd., San Jose, California, 1960).
26. Chapin, H. and Smith, F. G. W., *The Ocean River* Victor Gollancz Ltd., London, 1953).
27. Churchward, J., *The Children of Mu* (Rider and Co., London, 1931).
28. Churchward, J., *The Lost Continent of Mu* (Rider and Co., London, 1931).
29. Colbert, E. H., *The Age of Reptiles* (Weidenfeld and Nicholson, London, 1965).
30. Collinder, P., *A History of Marine Navigation* (B. T. Batsford Ltd., London, 1954).
31. Cousteau, J. Y., *World Without Sun* (William Heinemann Ltd., London, 1965).
32. Cousteau, J. Y. and Dugan, J., *Captain Cousteau's Underwater Treasury* (Hamish Hamilton, London, 1960).
33. Cousteau, J. Y. and Dugan, J., *The Living Sea* (Hamish Hamilton, London, 1963).
34. Cousteau, J. Y. and Dumas, F., *The Silent World* (Hamish Hamilton, London, 1953).
35. Cowburn, P., *The Warship in History* (Macmillan and Co. Ltd., London, 1966).
36. Cromie, W. J., *Exploring the Secrets of the Sea* (George Allen and Unwin Ltd., London, 1964).
37. Daly, R. A., *The Changing World of the Ice Age* (Yale University Press, New Haven, 1934).
38. Daly, R. A., *The Floor of the Ocean* (University of North Carolina Press, Durham, N. Carolina, 1945).
39. Darwin, F., *The Life and Letters of Charles Darwin* (John Murray, London, 1887).
40. Davis, R. H., *Breathing in Irrespirable Atmospheres* (The Saint Catherine Press Ltd., London, 1948).

41. Davis, R. H., *Deep Diving and Submarine Operations* (Siebe, Gorman and Co. Ltd., London, 1962).
42. Davis, S. N. and DeWiest, R. J. M., *Hydrogeology* (John Wiley and Sons Inc., New York, 1966).
43. Deacon, G. E. R., Ed., *Oceans* (Paul Hamlyn, London, 1968).
44. Diolé, P., *4000 Years Under the Sea* (Sidgewick and Jackson Ltd., London, 1954).
45. Diolé, P., *The Undersea Adventure* (Sidgewick and Jackson Ltd., London, 1953).
46. Diolé, P., *Under-water Exploration* (Elek Books Ltd., London, 1954).
47. Donnelly, I., *Atlantis: The Antediluvian World* (Sidgewick and Jackson Ltd., London, 1960).
48. Dugan, J., *Man Explores the Sea* (Hamish Hamilton, London, 1956).
49. Dugan, J., *Undersea Explorer* (Hamish Hamilton, London, 1957).
50. Dumas, F., *Deep-Water Archaeology* (Routledge and Kegan Paul, London, 1962).
51. Dumas, F., *Épaves Antiques* (G. P. Maisonneuve et Larose, Paris, 1964).
52. Dunbar, C. C., *The Earth* (Weidenfeld and Nicholson, London, 1966).
53. Dunbar, J., *The Lost Land* (Collins, London, 1958).
54. Fisher, J., *Nature* (Macdonald and Co. [Publishers] Ltd., London, 1960).
55. Florkin, M., Ed., *Aspects of the Origin of Life* (Pergamon Press, London, 1960).
56. Forster, E. M., *Alexandria* (Doubleday and Co. Inc., New York, 1961).
57. Franklin, B., *Autobiography* (Hutchinson and Co., London, 1903).
58. Franzen, A., *The Warship Vasa* (P. A. Norstedt and Sons, Stockholm, 1962).
59. Fraser, R., *The Habitable Earth* (Hodder and Stoughton Ltd., London, 1964).
60. Frost, H., *Under the Mediterranean* (Routledge and Kegan Paul, London, 1963).
61. Gaskell, T. F., *World Beneath the Oceans* (Aldus Books Ltd., London, 1964).
62. Gilpatric, G., *The Compleat Goggler* (John Lane The Bodley Head Ltd., London, 1939).
63. Glob, P. V., *The Bog People* (Faber and Faber, London, 1969).

64. Gross, M. G., *Oceanography* (Charles E. Merrill Books Inc., Columbus, Ohio, 1967).
65. Guilcher, A., *Coastal and Submarine Morphology* (Methuen and Co. Ltd., London, 1958).
66. Haldane, J. S., and Priestly, J. G., *Respiration* (Oxford University Press, London, 1935).
67. Halstead, B. W., *Dangerous Marine Animals* (Cornell Maritime Press, Cambridge, Md., U.S.A. 1959).
68. Hass, H., *Under the Red Sea* (Jarrolds Publishers [London] Ltd., London, 1952).
69. Heiskanen, W. A., and Meinesz, F. A. V., *The Earth and its Gravity Field* (McGraw–Hill Book Co. Inc., New York, 1958).
70. Hencken, H. O'N., *The Archaeology of Cornwall and Scilly* (Methuen & Co. Ltd., London, 1932).
71. Herodotus, *History* (John Murray, London, 1880).
72. Hitti, P. K., *History of Syria* (Macmillan and Co. Ltd., London, 1951).
73. Holmes, A., *Principles of Physical Geology* (Thomas Nelson and Sons Ltd., London, 1965).
74. Holmes, D. L., *Elements of Physical Geology* (Thomas Nelson and Sons Ltd., London, 1969).
75. Homer, *The Iliad* (Penguin Books Ltd., Harmondsworth, 1950).
76. Homer, *The Odyssey* (Penguin Books Ltd., Harmondsworth, 1951).
77. Houot, G. and Willm., P., *Two Thousand Fathoms Down* (Hamish Hamilton and Rupert Hart-Davis, London, 1955).
78. Houston, J. M., *The Western Mediterranean World* (Longmans, Green and Co. Ltd., London, 1964).
79. Ibn Battuta, *Travels in Asia and Africa* (George Routledge and Sons Ltd., London, 1929).
80. King, C. A. M., *Techniques in Geomorphology* (Edward Arnold [Publishers] Ltd., London, 1967).
81. King, L. C., *The Morphology of the Earth* (Oliver and Boyd, Edinburgh, 1962).
82. King, T., *Water* (The Macmillan Co., New York, 1953).
83. Huenen, P. H., *Realms of Water* (Cleaver–Hume Press Ltd., London, 1955).
84. Kurten, B., *Pleistocene Mammals of Europe* (Weidenfeld and Nicholson, London, 1968).
85. Lane, F. C., *The Mysterious Sea* (Sampson Low, Marston and Co. Ltd., London, 1949).

86. Larsen, E., *Men Under the Sea* (Phoenix House Ltd., London, 1960).
87. Latil, P. de and Rivoire, J., *Man and the Underwater World* (Jarrolds Publishers [London] Ltd., London, 1956).
88. Latil, P. de and Rivoire, J., *Sunken Treasure* (Rupert Hart-Davis, London, 1962).
89. Lauring, P., *Land of the Tollund Man* (Lutterworth Press, London, 1957).
90. Lavaur, G. de, *Caves and Cave Diving* (Robert Hale Ltd., London, 1956).
91. Lee, O., *Complete Illustrated Guide to Snorkel and Deep Diving* (Doubleday and Co. Inc., New York, 1963).
92. MacPike, E. F., Ed., *Correspondence and Papers of Edmund Halley* (Oxford University Press, London, 1932).
93. Magnus, O., *Historia de gentibus Septentrionalibus* (J. M. de Viottis, Rome, 1555).
94. Marx, R. F., *Pirate Port* (Pelham Books Ltd., London, 1968).
95. Marx, R. F., *They Dared the Deep* (Pelham Books Ltd., London, 1968).
96. Miles, S., *Underwater Medicine* (Staples Press, London, 1962).
97. Moore, R. C., *Introduction to Historical Geology* (McGraw-Hill Book Co. Inc., New York, 1958).
98. Muck, O. H., *Atlantis-Gefunden* (Victoria Verlag, Stuttgart, 1955).
99. Munro, R., *The Lake-Dwellings of Europe* (Cassell and Co. Ltd., London, 1890).
100. Myres, J. L., *Who Were the Greeks?* (University of California Press, Berkeley, 1930).
101. Ohrelius, B., *VASA, The King's Ship* (Cassell and Co. Ltd., London, 1962).
102. Ordway, R. J., *Earth Science* (D. van Nostrand Co., Inc., Princeton, N.J., 1966).
103. Ovid, *Metamorphoses* (William Heinemann Ltd., London, 1958).
104. Pausanias, *Description of Greece* (Macmillan and Co. Ltd., London, 1898).
105. Peterson, M., *History Under the Sea* (Smithsonian Institution Press, Washington, 1969).
106. Petrie, W. M. F., *Methods and Aims in Archaeology* (Macmillan and Co. Ltd., London, 1904).
107. Plato, *Timaeus* (William Heinemann Ltd., London, 1929).
108. Pliny, *Historia Naturalis* (William Heinemann Ltd., London, 1938).

109. Plongeon, A. le, *Queen Móo and the Egyptian Sphinx* (Redding and Co., New York, 1900).
110. Polybius, *Histories* (Macmillan and Co., London, 1889).
111. Poulet, G., *Newnes Complete Guide to Underwater Swimming* (George Newnes Ltd., London, 1964).
112. Proudman, J., *Dynamical Oceanography* (Methuen and Co., London, 1953).
113. Quilici, F., *The Blue Continent* (Weidenfeld and Nicolson, London, 1954).
114. Raitt, H., *Exploring the Deep Pacific* (Staples Press Ltd., London, 1957).
115. Ray, C. and Ciampi, E., *The Underwater Guide to Marine Life* (Nicholas Kaye Ltd., London, 1958).
116. Rebikoff, D., *Free Diving* (Sidgewick and Jackson, London, 1955).
117. Rebikoff, D., *Underwater Photography* (The American Photographic Book Publishing Co. Inc., New York, 1965).
118. Roghi, G. and Baschieri, F., *Dahlak* (Nicholas Kaye, London, 1956).
119. Rose, J. H., *Man and the Sea* (W. Heffer and Sons Ltd., Cambridge, 1935).
120. Runcorn, S. K., Ed., *Continental Drift* (Academic Press Inc. [London] Ltd., London, 1962).
121. Saunders, R., *The Raising of the Vasa* (Oldbourne Book Co. Ltd., London, 1962).
122. Schaefer, K. E., Ed., *Man's Dependence on the Earthly Atmosphere* (The Macmillan Co., New York, 1962).
123. Scott-Elliot, W., *The Story of Atlantis and the Lost Lemuria* (The Theosophical Publishing House London Ltd., London, 1932).
124. Shepard, F. P., *Submarine Geology* (Harper and Row, New York, 1963).
125. Smiles, S., *Harbours-Lighthouses-Bridges* (John Murray, London, 1874).
126. Spence, L., *The Problem of Lemuria* (Rider and Co., London, 1932).
127. Stenuit, R., *The Deepest Days* (Hodder and Stoughton Ltd., London, 1966).
128. Strabo, *The Geography* (William Heinemann, London, 1923).
129. Suess, F. E., *The Face of the Earth* (Oxford University Press, London, 1904–24).
130. Sweeney, J., *Skin Diving and Exploring Underwater* (Frederick Muller Ltd., London, 1956).

131. Swinton, W. E., *The Corridor of Life* (Jonathan Cape, London, 1948).

132. Tacitus, *Annals* (John Norton, London, 1612).

133. Tailliez, P., *Aquarius* (George G. Harrap and Co., Ltd., London, 1964).

134. Taylor, J. du P., Ed., *Marine Archaeology* (Hutchinson and Co., [Publishers] Ltd., London, 1965).

135. Thompson, E. H., *People of the Serpent* (Houghton Mifflin Co., New York, 1932).

136. Throckmorton, P., *The Lost Ships* (Jonathan Cape, London, 1965).

137. Thucydides, *The Peloponnesian War* (University of Michigan Press, Ann Arbor, 1959).

138. Toit, A. du, *Our Wandering Continents* (Oliver and Boyd Ltd., Edinburgh, 1937).

139. Ucelli, G., *Le Navi de Nemi* (La Libreria dello Stato, Rome, 1950).

140. Verrill, A. H., *They Found Gold* (G. P. Putnam's Sons, New York, 1936).

141. Vine, A. E. and Rees, N., *Plant and Animal Biology* (Sir Isaac Pitman and Son Ltd., London, 1968).

142. Vita-Finzi, C., *The Mediterranean Valleys* (Cambridge University Press, Cambridge, 1969).

143. Vyvyan, C. C., *The Scilly Isles* (Robert Hale Ltd., London, 1953).

144. Wace, A. J. B. and Stubbings, F. H., Eds., *A Companion to Homer* (Macmillan and Co. Ltd., London, 1962).

145. Wegener, A., *The Origin of Continents and Oceans* (Methuen and Co. Ltd., London, 1966).

146. Wilkins, J., *Mathematicall Magick* (Sa. Gellibrand, London, 1648).

147. Willard, T. A., *The City of the Sacred Well* (William Heinemann Ltd., London, 1926).

148. Williamson, James A., *The English Channel* (Collins, London, 1959).

149. Woolley, Leonard, *Excavations at Ur* (Ernest Benn Ltd., London, 1954).

150. Wright, T., *Early Travels in Palestine* (Henry G. Bohn, London, 1848).

151. Young, D., *The Man in the Helmet* (Cassell and Co., Ltd., London, 1963).

152. Zeuner, F. E., *Dating the Past* (Methuen and Co. Ltd., London, 1958).

Index